W. H. AUDEN

The Age of
Anxiety

W. H. AUDEN: CRITICAL EDITIONS

GENERAL EDITOR

Edward Mendelson

Lectures on Shakespeare
Reconstructed and edited by
Arthur Kirsch

Juvenilia: Poems, 1922–1928
Expanded Paperback Edition
Edited by Katherine Bucknell

The Sea and the Mirror
A Commentary on Shakespeare's The Tempest
Edited by Arthur Kirsch

The Age of Anxiety
A Baroque Eclogue
Edited by Alan Jacobs

W. H. AUDEN

The Age of Anxiety

* * *

A Baroque Eclogue

EDITED BY

Alan Jacobs

PRINCETON UNIVERSITY PRESS
PRINCETON AND OXFORD

Published by Princeton University Press, 41 William Street,
Princeton, New Jersey 08540
In the United Kingdom: Princeton University Press, 6 Oxford Street,
Woodstock, Oxfordshire OX20 1TW
press.princeton.edu

Jacket illustration: W. H. Auden on the beach in 1946 (photo by Jerry Cooke).
Time & Life Pictures/Getty Images

Library of Congress Cataloging-in-Publication Data

Auden, W. H. (Wystan Hugh), 1907–1973.
The age of anxiety : a baroque eclogue / W.H. Auden ; edited by Alan Jacobs.
p. cm. — (W.H. Auden : critical editions)
Originally published: New York : Random House, 1947.
An annotated critical edition of Auden's last, longest book-length poem.
Includes bibliographical references.
ISBN 978-0-691-13815-2 (acid-free paper) 1. Anxiety—Poetry. 2. Civilization,
Modern—20th century—Poetry. I. Jacobs, Alan, 1958– II. Title.
PR6001.U4A65 2011
821'.914—dc22
2010020433

British Library Cataloging-in-Publication Data is available

This book has been composed in ITC New Baskerville
Printed on acid-free paper. ∞
Printed in the United States of America
5 7 9 10 8 6

CONTENTS

PREFACE
vii

INTRODUCTION
xi

The Age of Anxiety
1

APPENDIX
Two Letters on Metrical Matters
109

TEXTUAL NOTES
113

PREFACE

I sit in one of the dives
On Fifty-Second Street
Uncertain and afraid . . .

So begins W. H. Auden's "September 1, 1939," a poem whose title re-
fers to the day that German armies invaded Poland, thus beginning
the Second World War. Five years later, as the war continued, Auden
began another poem that also opens in a New York bar and in the
same mood of doubt and fear. The location is now a bar on Third
Avenue, and four characters are present, not just a single authorial
voice. Moreover, if the earlier poem ended more or less where it
began, though with a desire to "show an affirming flame" in the face
of a new war's fears, this later, far longer one takes its characters
through vast tracts of imaginative space before releasing them to their
daily lives.

In early drafts of *The Age of Anxiety* the four are called, simply, Civil-
ian, Doctor, Girl, and Merchant Seaman. Later they would become a
shipping clerk, Quant; a medical intelligence officer in the Canadian
Air Force, Malin; a department-store buyer, Rosetta; and a recently
enlisted navy man, Emble. All four are in a sense displaced persons, as
Auden himself had been since January 1939, when he arrived in
America from England. Quant was born in Ireland, Rosetta in En-
gland; Malin is Canadian, and even Emble, the one native-born Amer-
ican, seems to be from the Midwest: he is certainly not a New Yorker.
But they are not distinctively uprooted. "In war-time," he writes in the
poem's Prologue, "everybody is reduced to the anxious status of a
shady character or a displaced person." And displacement inevitably
produces anxiety.

Perhaps because of their shared displacement, the four understand
that they together inhabit a region of space and a moment of time. In

this respect they differ from the speaker of "September 1, 1939," whose anxieties are solitary, though he sits in a crowded bar. What they go through together echoes—imperfectly—something that had happened to Auden himself in his midtwenties, when he was teaching at the Downs School, Colwall:

> One fine summer night in June 1933 I was sitting on a lawn after dinner with three colleagues, two women and one man. . . . We were talking casually about everyday matters when, quite suddenly and unexpectedly, something happened. I felt myself invaded by a power which, though I consented to it, was irresistible and certainly not mine. For the first time in my life I knew exactly—because, thanks to the power, I was doing it—what it means to love one's neighbor as oneself. I was also certain, though the conversation continued to be perfectly ordinary, that my three colleagues were having the same experience. (In the case of one of them, I was later able to confirm this.) My personal feelings towards them were unchanged—they were still colleagues, not intimate friends—but I felt their existence as themselves to be of infinite value and rejoiced in it.

His poem "Out on the lawn I live in bed" emerged from this experience; though when he had the experience, and when he wrote the poem, he did not know what to make of it. Will these four—not even colleagues, much less intimate friends—discover a similar union?

I AM GRATEFUL to Edward Mendelson, general editor of this series, for extensive advice and counsel at every stage of this project.

Arthur Kirsch's edition of *The Sea and the Mirror* has been the model for my work here; I am thankful for that example. And I might add that I learned a great deal from Arthur when I took a class in Shakespeare from him many years ago, when I was a graduate student at the University of Virginia. There are many other Auden scholars who have been my teachers-at-a-distance, but I must single out John Fuller, whose *W. H. Auden: A Commentary* served to orient me to this poem when I thought I might well never come to terms with it.

The staff at the Harry Ransom Center at the University of Texas at Austin, the Beinecke Library at Yale University, the Harvard University Archives, and the Henry W. and Albert A. Berg Collection of English and American Literature at the New York Public Library were unfailingly helpful and cordial.

Finally, I am greatly indebted to my assistant Aubrey Buster, who gave extensive aid in the typing of the poem and the collecting of multiple editions. Aubrey does this kind of hard work with remarkable skill and even more remarkable cheerfulness; the task of producing this volume would have been much more painful and time-consuming had I not had her assistance.

INTRODUCTION

THE POEM

The Age of Anxiety begins in fear and doubt, but the four protagonists find some comfort in sharing their distress. In even this accidental and temporary community there arises the possibility of what Auden once called "local understanding." Certain anxieties may be overcome not by the altering of geopolitical conditions but by the cultivation of mutual sympathy—perhaps mutual love, even among those who hours before had been strangers.

The Age of Anxiety is W. H. Auden's last book-length poem, his longest poem, and almost certainly the least-read of his major works. ("It's frightfully long," he told his friend Alan Ansen.) It would be interesting to know what fraction of those who begin reading it persist to the end. The poem is strange and oblique; it pursues in a highly concentrated form many of Auden's long-term fascinations. Its meter imitates medieval alliterative verse, which Auden had been drawn to as an undergraduate when he attended J.R.R. Tolkien's lectures in Anglo-Saxon philology, and which clearly influences the poems of his early twenties. *The Age of Anxiety* is largely a psychological, or psychohistorical, poem, and these were the categories in which Auden preferred to think in his early adulthood (including his undergraduate years at Oxford, when he enjoyed the role of confidential amateur analyst for his friends).

The poem also embraces Auden's interest in, among other things, the archetypal theories of Carl Gustav Jung, Jewish mysticism, English murder mysteries, and the linguistic and cultural differences between England and America. Woven through it is his nearly lifelong obsession with the poetic and mythological "green world" Auden variously calls Arcadia or Eden or simply the Good Place. Auden's previous long poem had been called "The Sea and the Mirror: A Commentary on Shakespeare's *The Tempest*," and Shakespeare haunts this poem too. (In the latter stages of writing *The Age of Anxiety* Auden was teaching a course on Shakespeare at the New School in Manhattan.)

But it should also be noted that this last long poem ended an era for Auden; his thought and verse pursued new directions after he completed it.

Many cultural critics over the decades—starting with Jacques Barzun in one of the earliest reviews—have lauded Auden for his acuity in naming the era in which we live. But given the poem's difficulty, few of them have managed to figure out precisely *why* he thinks our age is characterized primarily by anxiety—or even whether he is really saying that at all. *The Age of Anxiety*, then, is extraordinarily famous for a book so little read; or, extraordinarily little read for a book so famous. The purpose of the current edition is to aid those who would like to read the poem rather than sagely cite its title.

AUDEN, WITH his friend Christopher Isherwood, had come to America in January of 1939. In April of that year he wrote to an American acquaintance, "I shall, I hope, be in the States for a year or so," but his estimate was quite mistaken. He spent more than two years in New York, during which he met a young man named Chester Kallman, soon to become his lover, and returned to the Anglican Christianity of his childhood. For a year he taught at the University of Michigan, then made his way to Swarthmore College in Pennsylvania, where he taught from 1942 to 1945. In July of 1944, while staying in the Manhattan apartment of his friends James and Tania Stern, he began writing this poem.

At the end of the next academic year, in April of 1945, Auden joined the Morale Division of the U.S. Strategic Bombing Survey. He had been recommended for this job by a fellow faculty member at Swarthmore, and then was actively recruited by a leading officer of the Survey. The purpose of the Survey was to understand what the Allied bombing campaigns had done to Germany; the Morale Division was especially concerned with psychological impact. Auden's public support of the war effort and his fluency in German made him an ideal candidate for this work. He was assigned the equivalent rank of Major and told to buy himself a uniform. In a surviving photograph he looks quite trim and neat in it, a significant departure from his habitual slovenliness. "I should have got along quite well in the Army," he told Alan Ansen.

The condition of Germany shocked and grieved Auden. In the ruined town of Darmstadt he wrote to his friend Elizabeth Mayer, herself German-born: "I keep wishing you were with us to help and then I think, perhaps not, for as I write this sentence I find myself crying." But it seems likely that during his work for the Survey he also came to understand more clearly the extent of the Nazis' devastation of German Jewry: *The Age of Anxiety* is among the first poems in English, perhaps the very first, to register the fact of the Nazis' genocidal murder of millions of Jews.

When Auden returned from Europe, he found the first of several apartments in Manhattan in which he lived almost until the end of his life. But this was an unsettled time for him. He taught the Shakespeare class without especially enjoying it: to a friend he wrote, "The Shakespeare course makes me despair. I have 500 students and so can do nothing but boom away." He worked, off and on, with Bertolt Brecht on an adaptation of *The Duchess of Malfi*. He taught for a term at Bennington College in Vermont, read prodigiously in many fields, and wrote dozens of reviews and essays for a wide range of American periodicals. A lifelong homosexual, he decided that he should have an affair with a woman, and did so. (It was in some respects a successful experiment, though not one that he chose to repeat, and he and Rhoda Jaffe remained on friendly terms afterward.) A decade later he would write, "At the age of thirty-seven"—his age when he began *The Age of Anxiety*—"I was still too young to have any sure sense of the direction in which I was moving." The poem testifies to Auden's confusions. But it also formulates an intellectually powerful response to them.

THE POEM begins with a man named Quant contemplating his reflection in a mirror. The mirror of "The Sea and the Mirror" had been the one that Hamlet says "playing" (acting) holds up to nature. That was fitting, for one of Auden's purposes in that poem was to describe what it is that poetry represents, or can represent, and what the purpose of such representation might be. But *The Age of Anxiety* is particularly concerned with a kind of mirroring indicated elsewhere in *Hamlet*, at the moment when the prince tells his mother, "You go not till I set you up a glass / Where you may see the inmost part of you." Can we see ourselves in any given mirror? Do reflections yield reliable knowledge, especially given that mirrors invert? "My deuce, my double, my dear image," the man muses, "Is it lively there" in "that land of glass"? "Does your self like mine / Taste of untruth? Tell me, what are you / Hiding in your heart"? (When I call what I see in the mirror my image or reflection, I am saying that it's not *me*.) A few lines after these meditations, we hear the thoughts of another character, Malin: "Man has no mean; his mirrors distort."

Auden thought often about mirrors in those days. He began a 1942 essay for the Roman Catholic weekly *Commonweal* with these words:

> Every child, as he wakes into life, finds a mirror underneath his pillow. Look in it he will and must, else he cannot know who he is, a creature fallen from grace, and this knowledge is a necessary preliminary to salvation. Yet at the moment he looks into his mirror, he falls into mortal danger, tempted by guilt into a despair which tells him that his isolation and abandonment is [*sic*] irrevocable. It is impossible to face such abandonment and live, but as long as he gazes into the mirror he need not face it; he has at least his mirror as an illusory companion. . . .

And in "For the Time Being," the long poem that preceded "The Sea and the Mirror," Auden writes of an ultimate existential dislocation in this way:

> It's as if
> We had left our house for five minutes to mail a letter,
> And during that time the living room had changed places
> With the room behind the mirror over the fireplace . . .

So as Quant observes his deuce, his double, his dear image, he is endangered by the "dearness"; but at least he recognizes that it is not his self; he is healthily distanced, at least to some degree, from it. He knows that the room in the mirror differs from the one he inhabits.

Much later in the poem Malin—who often, though not always, speaks for Auden—will designate "The police, / The dress-designers, etc." as those "who manage the mirrors." That is, the images of ourselves that we typically see are controlled by political and commercial forces. One might say that ideology is the construction and presentation of mirrors to meet certain predetermined purposes, none of which is the valid self-understanding of the viewer.

Though the events of the poem take place during the war, the writing of it continued once the war was over, and Auden is at considerable pains to show that the anxieties exacerbated by wartime do not evaporate when war ends. Indeed, often just the opposite happens: in her book *Between Past and Future* (1954) Hannah Arendt—who knew Auden well late in life, though she first met him when he was writing this poem—describes the sense of emptiness, the loss of meaning, experienced by those who had resisted the Nazis once the Nazis were defeated. The enemy vanquished, the anxieties remain, and are thereby revealed to have their source in something other than the immediacy of wartime fears.

Auden explores this point comically in "Under Which Lyre: A Reactionary Tract for the Times," the only other poem he completed while he was working on *The Age of Anxiety*. Now that "Ares has quit the field" a new conflict emerges:

> Let Ares doze, that other war
> Is instantly declared once more
>   'Twixt those who follow
> Precocious Hermes all the way
> And those who without qualms obey
>   Pompous Apollo. . . .
>
> The sons of Hermes love to play
> And only do their best when they
>   Are told they oughtn't;
> Apollo's children never shrink
> From boring jobs but have to think
>   Their work important.

The followers of Hermes pursue art and culture for their own sakes, or for pleasure; the followers of Apollo wish to rationalize culture, to systematize it and render it productive and efficient. Auden and his fellow Hermetics do not wish to rule—"The earth would soon, did Hermes run it, / Be like the Balkans"—but rather to be left alone. However, the deep Apollonian suspicion of unconstrained and unjustified activities may not allow that to happen.

The same concerns are presented in a much more serious way in *The Age of Anxiety*. Malin again:

> But the new barbarian is no uncouth
> Desert-dweller; he does not emerge
> From fir forests; factories bred him;
> Corporate companies, college towns
> Mothered his mind, and many journals
> Backed his beliefs.

The "new barbarian" is also the manager of our mirrors; which means that though "Ares has left the field" we cannot take our ease, because we cannot be confident that we know ourselves sufficiently well to discern the managers' manipulations. As a third character in *The Age of Anxiety*, Rosetta, says, "Lies and lethargies police the world / In its periods of peace." Moreover, she laments,

> . . . life after life lapses out of
> Its essential self and sinks into
> One press-applauded public untruth
> And, massed to its music, all march in step
> Led by that liar, the lukewarm Spirit
> Of the Escalator

—the Spirit of of the Escalator being that Apollonian demi-deity who personifies irresistible Progress, the move ever upward. Our cultural world is increasingly dominated by Apollo: his voice emerges even from the jukebox that we hear often in this poem. That same voice is evoked in "Under Which Lyre":

> His [Apollo's] radio Homers all day long
> In over-Whitmanated song
>   That does not scan,
> With adjectives laid end to end,
> Extol the doughnut and commend
>   The Common Man.

(The moment in the poem when Quant points a finger at the radio and thereby silences it was surely, for Auden, a wish-fulfillment dream.) In such an environment—with our mirrors distorted by internal and external forces alike—how can we hope to find what Hamlet proposed to show Gertrude, a glass in which we can see the inmost part of ourselves?

The models of psychoanalysis devised by Freud and his successors promise such a mirror. Early in his career Auden was deeply Freudian in his thinking, and when Freud died in 1939 Auden wrote a memorial poem that is largely an encomium, with reservations emerging only near the poem's end: "If often he was wrong and, at times, absurd," nevertheless he has become "a whole climate of opinion." But soon thereafter Auden's skepticism would become more overt: in his 1942 *Commonweal* essay he wrote,

> Psychoanalysis, like all pagan *scientia*, says, "Come, my good man, no wonder you feel guilty. You have a distorting mirror, and that is indeed a very wicked thing to have. But cheer up. For a trifling consideration I shall be delighted to straighten it out for you. There. Look. A perfect image. The evil of distortion is exorcised. Now you have nothing to repent of any longer. Now you are one of the illumined and elect. That will be ten thousand dollars, please.
>
> And immediately come seven devils, and the last state of that man is worse than the first.

This is a severe critique, coming from someone for whom Freud had been so central a figure. And it is strange to see Auden treating psychoanalysis so skeptically, since at the very time he wrote those words he was drawing regularly—especially in his verse—on the work of Carl Gustav Jung.

But while Auden made use of what he found in Jung he was never devoted to him, as he had been devoted to Freud. Freud was for the young Auden primarily, supremely, a healer—in the elegy he is first referred to as "this doctor"—and then a teacher: he taught the present self "how rich life had been and how silly," and thereby enabled that self to become "life-forgiven and more humble." When Auden came to question Freud's stature as healer and teacher alike, he never granted Jung the honor he had granted Freud. Instead, he discovered in Jung a rich conceptual vocabulary that could be applied to many of Auden's own key concerns. Jung's account of myth and archetype would provide a way for Auden to talk about the power of poetry and story for the rest of his life. Throughout the decade of the forties, Auden would draw heavily on Jung's model of psychological types;

and this would be Jung's primary contribution—and that of modern psychology—to *The Age of Anxiety*.

In 1921 Jung published *Psychologische Typen* (Psychological Types), in which he created a series of binary categories. He opposed the *extravert*, for whom social interaction is a source of energy, to the *introvert*, who loses energy through social interaction. He claimed that some of us perceive the world primarily through *sensation*, others through *intuition*; and that some of us make our ethical judgments primarily through *thinking*, others through *feeling*. (These distinctions became widely known when they were adapted for the Myers-Briggs Type Indicator tests administered in many workplaces.) Auden, an inveterate maker of charts and diagrams, was powerfully drawn to such schematic categories. The introvert/extravert dichotomy doesn't show up often in his work, but the rest of Jung's typology makes its first appearance in "For the Time Being" in the section called "The Four Faculties." There the faculties introduce themselves in this way:

> INTUITION As a dwarf in the dark of
>   His belly I rest;
> FEELING A nymph, I inhabit
>   The heart in his breast;
> SENSATION A giant, at the gates of
>   His body I stand;
> THOUGHT His dreaming brain is
>   My fairyland.

So Intuition abides in the belly—whence we get our "gut instinct"— while Feeling's traditional home is the heart; Sensation depends on the five senses, while Thought trusts the workings of the brain. (In Jung's account, each of these can be experienced in an introverted or extraverted mode. Auden leaves out that complication.)

The Four Faculties really have nothing to do with what happens in "For the Time Being": it appears that Auden was simply fascinated by this schema and was determined to shoehorn it in. (Later in life he

questioned his own judgment: in 1963 he wrote in the margin of this
passage in a copy of "For the Time Being," "Bosh, straight from Jung.")
But *The Age of Anxiety* contains a much more serious and thorough-
going attempt to appropriate the Jungian types and set them in mean-
ingful interrelation.

That each of the poem's characters represents one of the Faculties
is clear. Quant is Intuition; Malin, Thought; Rosetta, Feeling; Emble,
Sensation. Their names indicate the connections more or less clearly.
Malin is the most straightforward: *malin*, in familiar French usage, means
"shrewd" or "knowing." Quant suggests a *quantum*—an indivisible unit—
and thus the Intuitive's tendency to grasp ideas and situations as
wholes. Emble calls forth "emblem," and in the seventeenth century
especially "emblem books" presented complex ideas in a single pic-
ture—that is, they made understanding possible through sight, one of
the senses. Rosetta may refer to the rose and its association with love
and therefore the heart, the site of feeling. (In "The Four Faculties"
Feeling is a "nymph," the only specifically female figure; that differ-
ence is made explicit in *The Age of Anxiety*.)

In "For the Time Being" the Four Faculties say,

> We who are four
> Were once but one,
> Before his act of
> Rebellion . . .

That is, the biblical Adam in the Garden of Eden, before the Fall,
perceived and judged with all his faculties equally: each of them func-
tioned perfectly, and each worked harmoniously with the others—
they formed a single apparatus of understanding.

But "his act of / Rebellion" changed all that: the faculties separated
and became competitive with one another. In one person Thought
hypertrophies while Intuition atrophies; in another the opposite is
true. Since, as the old *New England Primer* encapsulated the theology
that Auden held at this time, "In Adam's Fall / We sinned all," no one

lives in whom the faculties are integrated and balanced. Or, to put the point in Malin's terms, "Man has no mean; his mirrors distort." If Freudian analysis is a sham, and Jung offers merely heuristic descriptions of our condition, is there any way, then, to undo the consequences of the Fall—to reintegrate the Faculties, to perfect our mirrors—and thereby to assuage our anxiety?

FOR AUDEN, this is, as he wrote in 1941 in an elegy for Henry James, "our predicament":

> That catastrophic situation which neither
> Victory nor defeat can annul; to be
>   Deaf yet determined to sing,
> To be lame and blind yet burning for the Great Good Place,
> To be radically corrupt yet mournfully attracted
>   By the Real Distinguished Thing.

One way to confront this predicament is to seek a return to an innocent past; another is to press forward to a perfected future. Auden called these opposing inclinations Arcadian and Utopian, and discerned in them a strict temperamental divide. (That divide plays a role as fundamental to his thought as is Jung's distinction between introverts and extraverts to the latter's beliefs, which may explain why Auden doesn't seem particularly interested in that aspect of Jung's typology.)

Auden consistently identified himself with the Arcadians, and he could be withering about Utopianism. His critique of the followers of Apollo in "Under Which Lyre"—again, the only other poem he completed while writing *The Age of Anxiety*—is largely a critique of Utopianism written with a sense of the occasion on which Auden would first read it aloud, at a Harvard Phi Beta Kappa ceremony during the 1946 commencement ceremonies. One of the dominant figures of American culture at that time was James Bryant Conant, Harvard's president, who was striving to modernize the university and transform it into a research powerhouse focused on science and technology. In the process he emphasized the humanities, especially the classics, far less than Harvard had done through much of its history. Auden told Alan Ansen, "When I was delivering my Phi Beta Kappa poem in Cambridge, I met Conant for about five minutes. 'This is the real enemy,' I thought to myself. And I'm sure he had the same impression about me." To Auden Conant was the "new barbarian"—bred from "factories . . . Corporate companies, college towns"—whom Malin fears.

Given Auden's position on the Arcadian/Utopian axis, then, it is perhaps surprising that *The Age of Anxiety* is less concerned with the social dangers produced by the Utopian than with the personal temptations facing the Arcadian. But this had been true in "The Sea and the Mirror" too: Arcadianism may have contributed much to Auden's mirror, but he knew that it had its own way of warping reflections. Rosetta is the chief Arcadian of *The Age of Anxiety*: her memory constantly draws her back to her English upbringing—or, rather, to an idealized and therefore distorted image of that upbringing. Indeed, nostalgic reminiscence for a lost English landscape ("From Seager's Folly / We beheld what was ours") is the burden of her first speech, and of several others. But by the end of the poem she has come to realize the falseness of those memories: she is aware that her God

> . . . won't pretend to
> Forget how I began, nor grant belief
> In the mythical scenes I make up
> Of a home like theirs, the Innocent Place where
> His Law can't look, the leaves are so thick.

Rosetta is Jewish; her God is the God of Israel; and her last great speech repeatedly refers to Israel's history of exile, captivity, and wilderness wandering—of homelessness, of being unable to return to the scene of past comfort and security. (And of course this history had just reached its terrifying nadir in the Nazis' destruction of Europe's Jews, to which Rosetta refers quite directly, in one of the most moving passages in the whole poem.) That the gates of Eden are guarded by angels with flaming swords; that there is really no place to hide from God what we have done; that "the Innocent Place" is forever lost—these are her realizations as her part in the poem draws to a close.

In the prose prologue to the poem Auden tells us that Rosetta's "favorite day-dream" was one in which she "conjured up, detail by detail, one of those landscapes familiar to all readers of English detective stories, those lovely innocent countrysides inhabited by charming eccentrics with independent means and amusing hobbies to whom, until the sudden intrusion of a horrid corpse onto the tennis court or into the greenhouse, work and law and guilt are just literary words." Auden was a great lover of detective stories—"if I have any work to do, I must be careful not to get hold of a detective story, for once I begin one, I cannot work or sleep till I have finished it"—and considered that he and his fellow addicts shared a distinctive trait: "I suspect that the typical reader of detective stories is, like myself, a person who suffers from a sense of sin." For Auden the classic detective story is a parable of the Fall and of our hopes for being restored to a state of innocence. The phrase "state of grace" recurs in Auden's treatment of the subject: the primary conceit of the detective story is that the whole society in which it takes place is innocent until an act of murder "precipitates a crisis" by destroying that innocence. This brings law into play, "and for a time all must live in its shadow, till the fallen one is identified. With his arrest, innocence is restored, and the law retires forever." (After listening to a radio report on the progress of the war, Malin's first thought is: "A crime has occurred, accusing all.")

One can see from this description—quoted from an essay Auden wrote during the composition of *The Age of Anxiety*, and which interprets Rosetta's daydream—that the detective story is a distinctively Arcadian form of wish-fulfillment dream. The Arcadian wants to see his or her ideal society as having been perfect and innocent; and (still more) wants to believe that that original state can be perfectly restored, can become again just what it was. In some of the earliest drafts of the poem (the ones in which the characters are identified simply as Civilian, Doctor, Girl, and Merchant Seaman) the poem's narrative was conceived of as a detective story. A brief outline reads,

The murder

The stories of the suspects

The exposure of their lies (contradiction and fresh evidence)

The discovery of the murderer.

The notion was abandoned but still echoes in the poem in various ways—not just in Rosetta's fantasy, but also in the great lament or "Dirge" of Part Four in which the characters dream of a great father figure—"some Gilgamesh or Napoleon, some Solon or Sherlock Holmes"—who can embody the Law, enforce its strictures, and thereby restore the society to its primal innocence.

These are, for the poet and his characters alike, enormously tempting fantasies. Their centrality to the poem accounts for its dedication to John Betjeman, a poet deeply sensitive to the Arcadian appeal of certain English places and landscapes, and, for one known as a "light" poet, capable of deceptively powerful presentations of his ideal worlds and the emotions they prompted in him. (Betjeman was a master of "topophilia," love of place, Auden believed, which requires a degree of "visual imagination" that Auden felt he lacked. "It is one of my constant regrets that I am too shortsighted, too much of a Thinking Type, to attempt this sort of poetry." Yet there is much topophilic verse in *The Age of Anxiety*.)

Equally important, the times and places dear to Betjeman were dear to Auden too: they shared a love of Victoriana when that period of English history was scorned by almost all their peers. "Betjeman is really the only person who really understands many of the things that are important to me. . . . That's really my world—bicycles and harmoniums." And, he added, "That's why he got" the dedication of *The Age of Anxiety*.

Primarily through Rosetta's reminiscences, Auden clearly and powerfully presents the appeal of this Victorian Eden—but equally clearly and powerfully identifies it as a fantasy: not truly historical, and not a legitimate way of resolving "our predicament." ("Betjeman is really a minor poet, of course," he told Ansen, and that judgment is rooted in Auden's perception that Betjeman failed to see that the world he so vividly imagined in his verse was, if partly real, also partly a nostalgic fantasy.) This is clear even in the characters' own descriptions of what they want, as in Rosetta's self-mocking wish: "may our luck find the / Regressive road to Grandmother's House." The Arcadian temptation is in the end just as deceptive as the Utopian one of the "new barbarians."

AUDEN HAD largely traditional views about women, so it is not surprising that he would associate the woman of this party with Feeling, with the heart. But it is surprising that he associates Rosetta so closely with himself. A few years before writing this poem he had told Stephen Spender that he was a pronounced "Thinking-Intuitive type," which should relegate Feeling to a clearly subordinate place; and yet the connections between Auden and Rosetta are obvious, and go well beyond their shared Arcadian passion for detective stories. She seems to have grown up in Birmingham, as did Auden; the landscapes she idealizes are largely associated with the Pennine range of northern England, which Auden often identified as his Eden. Moreover, partly as a result of his experimental heterosexual affair with Rhoda Jaffe—who was Jewish and who in other respects likely served as a model for Rosetta—Auden was reading deeply in Jewish thought in this period and told friends that he was contemplating converting to Judaism.

But Auden remained a Christian, and if some of his interests and traits are refracted through Rosetta, others are manifest in Malin. Though Malin's outer life seems to have been based on that of John Thompson, a Canadian medical intelligence officer whom Auden met during the war and with whom he became friends, Auden himself was also interested in science and medicine—his father was a physician, and his early interests were almost wholly scientific and technical. He had even gone up to Oxford planning to read in the sciences. Malin is also the one Christian among the four characters of the poem, and near the end Auden gives him a long meditative reflection on the God of Jesus Christ that echoes Rosetta's preceding, still longer, and distinctively Jewish meditation; the two soliloquies are the clearly matching bookends of the poem's concluding pages.

(In his long poems of the forties Auden becomes less and less straightforward about expressing his Christian beliefs. "For the Time Being" is openly biblical and deeply theological; "The Sea and the Mirror," though its prime subject is the relationship between Christianity and Art, never directly mentions God; and *The Age of Anxiety* is virtually without religious reference until its closing pages. In later life he would often say, "Orthodoxy is reticence," but even as he was working on *The Age of Anxiety* he wrote in an introduction to a collection of Betjeman's poems that in "this season, the man of good will will wear his heart up his sleeve, not on it.")

As for Quant and Emble, Auden suggests that their innermost lives are largely closed to him. The poem leaves Emble passed out on Rosetta's bed, the first of the four to fall silent. Given the small role that Sensation played in Auden's psychological makeup, this cannot be surprising; but Quant, as Auden's fellow Intuitive, might be expected to play a significant role at the end. Yet with a brief comment on his stumble at the door of his house, in a "camp" idiom Auden enjoyed— "Why, Miss *ME*, what's the matter?"—"he opened his front door and disappeared." Thus Auden gives over the substance of the closing sections to Thinking and Feeling.

So two speak at length; one disappears with a joke; one is unconscious. The Four Faculties do not become, again, One; they remain separate and disproportionate. It might not be immediately obvious why the poem brings them together at all.

IN FACT, though, the four have embarked on a joint quest—more than one quest, perhaps. It would be helpful at this point to have an overview of the structure of the poem. It has six parts:

Part One: Prologue
Part Two: The Seven Ages
Part Three: The Seven Stages
Part Four: The Dirge
Part Five: The Masque
Part Six: Epilogue

The Prologue introduces us to the characters and introduces them to each other. At Rosetta's suggestion, they move from the bar to a booth so that they might "Consider . . . the incessant Now of / The traveler through time." What does it mean to be a human being living temporally? This question leads to Part Two, The Seven Ages.

The reference, of course, is to the famous speech by Jaques in Shakespeare's *As You Like It*. Malin, the clear leader here, introduces each Age in language that echoes and revises that of Jaques: "At first, the infant, / Mewling and puking in the nurse's arms" becomes "Behold the infant, helpless in cradle and / Righteous still"; at the end, Jaques's "second childishness and mere oblivion, / Sans teeth, sans eyes, sans taste, sans everything" is revised thus:

> His last chapter has little to say.
> He grows backward with gradual loss of
> Muscular tone and mental quickness . . .

But while Jaques delivers his picture of human development and decline as a monologue, Malin's introductions of the Ages—most of which are longer than Jacques's whole speech—generate responses from each of the other characters, who find in Malin's word-pictures opportunities for disagreement or alteration or addition, in registers of fear or excitement or despair. Auden's version of the Seven Ages is thoroughly polyphonic and is the means by which these characters first begin to emerge as distinct types. (The means of characterization here, and throughout much of the poem, are not those of the novelist but rather those of the taxonomic psychologist, and this is an ancient tradition: more than two thousand years before Jung, Theophrastus wrote *On Moral Characters*, the first extant set of "character sketches": the Faultfinder, the Talkative Man, the Slanderer. Similar modes of characterization are common in medieval poetry and drama, from Prudentius's *Psychomachia* to *Everyman*. Auden's practice here is far closer to Theophrastus or *Everyman* than to Tolstoy.)

As they meditate on their tour of each human being's personal history, the four realize that they have further exploration to do together. It is Quant who, after another glimpse of his image in the bar's mirror, decrees that Rosetta ("peregrine nymph") must be the one to lead them in this quest for understanding:

> O show us the route
> Into hope and health; give each the required
> Pass to appease the superior archons;
> Be our good guide.

And so they enter, together, a kind of dream vision. This is Part Three, the Seven Stages, which Auden introduces in this way: "So it was now as they sought that state of prehistoric happiness which, by human beings, can only be imagined in terms of a landscape bearing a symbolic resemblance to the human body."

Already there are difficulties. Is it really true that a "state of prehistoric happiness"—that Arcadian vision once more—"can *only* be imagined in terms of a landscape bearing a symbolic resemblance to the human body"? If so, why? No explanations are forthcoming. And as the reader joins the characters in moving through this landscape, it is often impossible to understand how what they see relates to the features of any human body we are familiar with. No wonder, as Edward Mendelson has commented, "the shape of the Edenic quest in 'The Seven Stages' has baffled even Auden's most sympathetic readers."

When Alan Ansen shared his own bafflement soon after the poem's publication, Auden professed surprise. He thought that by adding the linking passages in prose that are dotted throughout the poem, he had done his readers a considerable favor. The symbolic structure of

"The Seven Stages," he said, is "really quite straightforward. . . . It's all done in the Zohar." It is hard not to suspect that Auden was pulling Ansen's leg, for surely he understood as well as anyone that little in the Zohar is straightforward.

The Zohar (or *The Book of Splendor*) is perhaps the greatest Jewish mystical text. It was written in the thirteenth century in Spain by Moses de León, who attributed the work to a second-century Palestinian rabbi, Shimon bar Yohai. Only a few concepts from this immensely variegated work are relevant to Auden's poem. The Zohar inherits from earlier Kabbalistic writings the notion of the ten *sefirot* or "lights"—attributes of God, emanations of his power and thought. But it goes further by associating each of the *sefirot* with some part of the human body: *Hesed* (Mercy) is linked with the right arm, *Hod* (Majesty) with the left leg, *Tiferet* (Beauty) with the torso, and so on.

In "The Seven Stages" Auden is not borrowing this structure so much as riffing on it. His *sefirot*, if we may call them that, are seven in number rather than ten, and seem to be not attributes of God but rather forms of human desire for the ideal and the innocent. By associating his scheme with the Zohar, Auden may be suggesting that all such quests are, ultimately, quests for God; but if so, this notion is but vaguely indicated. The poet seems to be working more generally in the painterly tradition of the *paysage moralisé* or "moralized landscape"—a conceit he knew very well. By superimposing this symbolic framework upon the Kabbalistic one of the body's *sefirot*, and then portraying the encounter with this imagined world as a kind of quest-narrative, Auden layers genre upon genre with extraordinarily rococo flourishes. "Really quite straightforward" indeed.

The development of "The Seven Stages" certainly follows the model of the quest-narrative but transforms that genre radically. In an essay he wrote while working on *The Age of Anxiety*, Auden offers an interesting overview of the various kinds of quest-narrative—fairy tale, Grail quest, and so forth—from which it seems clear that the proper variety for "The Seven Stages" is the "Dream Quest": "The purpose of the journey is no object but spiritual knowledge, a vision of the reality behind appearances, [by which] the dreamer when he wakes can henceforth live his life on earth." The other kinds of quest may have some role to play in the poem, but this seems to be the chief model. Yet this dream constantly verges on nightmare. The landscapes here are as unsettling and ambiguous as those confronted by Browning's protagonist in "Childe Roland to the Dark Tower Came" (a poem Auden surely had in mind as he wrote), but this is not a solitary quest. The four friends—we may now call them that—are able to converse with one another, to share impressions of their temporary world. And yet they do not experience a common vision. In the Zohar the rabbis and their conversational partners tend to be of one mind and one heart; again and again Moses de León's characters are overwhelmed by a sense of gratitude for being able to participate in such enlightening conversation. Not so Quant and Malin and Rosetta and Emble. One by one they describe what confronts them, and it is often difficult to know whether they are experiencing the same thing: is the "tacit tarn" Rosetta sees identical with the "salt lake lapping" Quant hears? Do Malin's "kettle moraines" surround the same body of water, or does he perceive a different landscape? Emble's vague statement that "The earth looks woeful and wet" offers little help.

As they proceed through their landscape, they twice split into pairs: first Rosetta and Emble separate from Quant and Malin; then, later, Quant goes with Rosetta and Malin with Emble. It is noteworthy that Malin and Rosetta never go together. The four travel, at various times, on foot and by car, by rail and through air, on a trolley car, on bicycles and a boat; near the end they run a race. In all this they have, the narrator says, "a common goal"; Rosetta calls it "our common hope" even as she decrees a temporary parting.

In this quest led by the "peregrine nymph," while none of the characters understand the full meaning of anything they encounter—any more than the reader does—their *feelings* come into harmony and perhaps even unison. This occurs even though their general inclinations do not fundamentally alter: in the race they run during the Seventh Stage, Auden writes that "as they run, their rival natures, by art comparing and compared, reveal themselves." But their shared experience, at this low point in their quest, is a vague awareness of being accused, of falling under some dire judgment—a judgment whose rightness they all acknowledge. (The point of the epigraph of the whole poem, from the *Dies Irae*, becomes sharper here.) Each confesses sins that, collectively, amount to a brief anatomy of pride. In a 1941 review of Reinhold Niebuhr's *The Nature and Destiny of Man*, Auden had written of "the temptation to sin, [which] is what the psychologist calls anxiety, and the Christian calls lack of faith." At this point the characters experience a reinterpretation of their own condition: what had been named psychologically as "anxiety" comes home as a moral and spiritual predicament, "the temptation to sin."

This is bad news, but not as bad as it sounds. These events take place—as Auden decided, or decided to inform his readers, just before sending the poem to the publisher—on "the night of All Souls." Auden had learned from the maverick historian Eugen Rosenstock-Huessy that the great significance of that date on the Church's calendar is that it acknowledges and celebrates the "universal democracy of sinners under judgment": Quant, Malin, Rosetta, and Emble have, more or less consciously, joined that democracy.

Each, having seen his or her innermost self with disturbing clarity, has the same impulse: to flee into the nearby forest to hide and reflect. (Similarly, Adam and Eve, after "their eyes were opened," "hid themselves from the presence of the LORD God amongst the trees of the garden.") They "vanish down solitary paths, with no guide but their sorrows, no companion but their own voices. Their ways cross and recross yet never once do they meet." And when they are finally reunited, it is only in order to confront their utter failure—and, still more important, the illusory nature of their whole quest. "Their journey has been one long flight" from the real world, and that world confronts them now. At this moment of sad recognition they awake and find themselves back in the bar.

Their cab ride from the bar to Rosetta's apartment—this is the action of Part Four, "The Dirge"—is therefore somber. They have learned that they cannot save themselves, that they have no resources by which they might be healed of their anxiety; but they also discern that they will not be saved by "some semi-divine stranger with super-human powers, some Gilgamesh or Napoleon, some Solon or Sher-lock Holmes." (It may well be that the war they are living through, which had been promoted in large part by the German cult of the *Führer*, has ended such dreams for them.) For the loss of that hope they utter a collective lamentation.

In light of these dismal events it is perhaps surprising that the ac-tion of Part Five, "The Masque," is an improvised and symbolic wed-ding ceremony. But, as the narrator tells us, "In times of war even the crudest kind of positive affection between persons seems extraordi-narily beautiful, a noble symbol of the peace and forgiveness of which the whole world stands so desperately in need." So even the "quite casual attraction" that has arisen between Emble and Rosetta "seemed and was of immense importance." The "and was" indicates that the narrator has no wish to dismiss this refuge: when there is meaning in nothing else there can be meaning in love. And all four desperately hope for this meaning to be real and strong, and to be the founda-tion—somehow—for the restoration of social order and the achieve-ment of "the millennial Earthly Paradise." Having abandoned, in light of the catastrophic failure of their quest for "that state of prehistoric happiness," the Arcadian return, they now become Utopians of the heart, seeking through love the positive energies necessary to achieve some future perfection. (Even, or especially, when those energies are deflected they have great creative potential: Auden was thinking of the power of sublimation when, in his elegy on Freud, he wrote of "Eros, builder of cities.")

But there is a reason Auden calls this part a masque: it is a piece of self-consciously artificial play-acting. Surely Quant knows this and laughs at it when he builds "a little altar of sandwiches" and "invoke[s] the Queen of love." Yet all four seem utterly committed to the ritual as it unfolds, and when Quant and Malin depart, their well-wishing is both sincere and superficial. It is a sign, perhaps, of how little progress they have made except in mutual affection. But that is, by Auden's lights, significant progress indeed.

That they are indeed "play-acting" in this scene lies near the heart of the matter. Auden told Theodore Spencer that one of his goals in this poem was "to devise a rhetoric which would reveal the great vice of our age which is that we are all not only 'actors' but know that we are (reduplicated Hamlets) and that it is only at moments, in spite of ourselves, and when we least expect it, that our real feelings break through." Thus the importance of what was at that stage in composition the epigraph to the entire poem, from the highly mannered comic novelist Ronald Firbank (1886–1926): "'Oh, Heaven help me,' she prayed, to be decorative and to do right.'" It could be said that the great challenge for the "reduplicated Hamlets" of this poem is to learn how to be decorative and do right.

Auden believed that certain vital spiritual truths could be expressed, indirectly, through comedy, in ways that would be impossible through more straightforward means. Thus he wrote of P. G. Wodehouse's character Jeeves, "So speaks comically—and in what other mode than the comic could it on earth truthfully speak?—the voice of Agape, of Holy Love." But this is an unusual notion; it is understandable that Theodore Spencer, reading a draft of the poem, objected to the quotation from Firbank as frivolous. To this protest Auden replied: "Reluctantly, I agree with you. The Firbank epigraph must go. I think it very serious but no one else will unless I write an essay to explain why." In the end he simply moved the epigraph to "The Masque," where, despite its apparent lack of fit with a section that ends with a meditation on the genocide of Europe's Jews, it properly belongs. (Only with this move did the quotation from the *Dies Irae* take its place at the head of the work.)

And Auden eventually wrote that essay: in 1961 he gave a radio talk on "Ronald Firbank and an Amateur World," in which he strove to explain the virtue of treating, as Firbank does, both religion and sex as *games*, as having a distinctive human value when played by amateurs. Games are characterized, in Auden's view, by their arbitrariness, their freedom from the constraints of necessity. "The Masque" is both a religious and a sexual game, exhilarating for the participants as long as it lasts. But when it ends, it leaves them in a mood of reflective self-assessment.

So, paradoxically, it is in the artificiality of game playing that we are most likely to be surprised by "our real feelings": we find them when we are patently not looking for them. But this "breaking through" of truth is an unpredictable experience, and the anxieties and illusions of daily life can quickly reclaim their sovereignty over us. Whether this meeting on "the night of All Souls" will make a significant difference to the lives of the four temporary friends cannot be known, but there is no reason to think that any of them will meet again. In the Epilogue we are told, "QUANT and MALIN, after expressing their mutual pleasure at having met, after exchanging addresses and promising to look each other up some time, had parted and immediately forgotten each other's existence."

Have they been altered by their shared visionary experience? Certainly by the poem's end they are less the Theophrastian types they seemed to be at the start and more individual—but in a distinctive sense of that word. In yet another essay written during the composition of *The Age of Anxiety*, Auden claimed that "The term 'individual' has two senses, and one must be careful in discussion to find out in which sense it is being used. In the realm of nature, 'individual' means to be something others are not, to have uniqueness: in the realm of spirit, it means to become what one wills, to have a self-determined history." It is not clear whether all of the characters in this poem have achieved *full* individuality, "in the realm of spirit," during the course of their evening, and there is no guarantee that anything they do achieve will last; but no careful reader of the poem will be content to see any of them as simply a Jungian type.

As noted earlier, in their last appearances in the poem, Emble sleeps on Rosetta's bed, and Quant disappears behind his door. But Rosetta and Malin—the first at the end of Part Five, and the second in the brief Epilogue—are left to face, with a frightened nakedness, their God. One and the same God, Auden would say, though worshipped under two Covenants: the characters' meditations rhyme closely. They are sinners in the hands of a God who may, or may not, be angry— whose love is often indistinguishable from anger—but who in any case cannot be evaded or deceived.

In 1942 Auden had written,

> The difference between a genuine Judaism and a genuine Christianity is like the difference between a young girl who has been promised a husband in a dream and a married woman who believes that she loves and is loved.
>
> The young girl knows that the decisively important thing has not yet happened to her, that her present life is therefore a period of anticipation, important not in itself but in its relation to the future. . . .
>
> To the married woman, on the other hand, the decisively important thing has already happened, and because of this everything in the present is significant. . . .

Few traces of this view—which depends on the belief that the coming of the Messiah is "the decisively important thing," a belief more central to Judaism as a religion with biblical roots than to Judaism as a modern cultural practice—remain in *The Age of Anxiety*. Rosetta's great speech is built around the idea that something utterly decisive happened long ago: a covenant made by the Lord God with the people of Israel. And what has happened since is the complex and painful working-out of a covenantal bond that seems to cause pain on both sides. (It is probably important that this meditation is the conclusion of "The Masque," which as we have seen focuses largely on the contrastingly trivial and ephemeral connection between Rosetta and Emble.) Rosetta's knowledge that the God of Israel never wavers in his commitment is as disturbing as it is reassuring: modifying one of Israel's great songs of consolation, Psalm 139, she thinks,

> Though I fly to Wall Street
> Or Publisher's Row, or pass out, or
> Submerge in music, or marry well,
> Marooned on riches, He'll be right there
> With His Eye upon me. Should I hide away
> My secret sins in consulting rooms,
> My fears are before Him; He'll find all,
> Ignore nothing.

Rosetta's soliloquy is full of biblical references, almost all of them to episodes of exile and captivity; and she acknowledges the most recent and horrific captivity under Nazi Germany. Wondering "who'll be left" at the end of a history of persecutions and pogroms, she can only sigh and repeat the ancient *Shema*: "Hear, O Israel: the Lord our God is one God."

Rosetta's speech is saturated by the details of history—her own and that of her people—but Malin's meditation is more philosophical. He is concerned with God's great abstractions: "His Good," "His Question," "His Truth." (As Auden wrote in a letter to a friend, Quant's "defence against the contemporary scene is to make it frivolous where Malin tries to see it sub specie aeternitate"—from the perspective of eternity.) Yet in substance his thoughts are identical to Rosetta's:

> In our anguish we struggle
> To elude Him, to lie to Him, yet His love observes
> His appalling promise; His predilection

> As we wander and weep is with us to the end,
> Minding our meanings, our least matter dear to Him . . .

These believers, then, share a discomfort and a consolation: discomfort that all the dark things they have just learned about themselves in their dream-quest are known, and known perfectly, by their God; and consolation that none of that diminishes the divine love. Having experienced with their two companions the transmutation of "anxiety" into "the temptation to sin," they take the further step their nonreligious companions could not: they recognize their own lack of faith and repent of it.

Near the end of "The Sea and the Mirror" Caliban conjures up a vision of "the greatest grandest opera rendered by a very provincial touring company indeed." The members of this company fail in every possible way, and do so spectacularly, but, Caliban says, it is at that moment that "we are blessed with that Wholly Other Life from which we are separated by an essential emphatic gulf. . . . It is just here, among the ruins and the bones, that we may rejoice in the perfected Work that is not ours." Something similar happens to Malin and Rosetta: in the emphatic failure of their Arcadian quest; in the recognition that no great "semi-divine stranger with superhuman powers" will arrive to rescue them; in the acknowledgment that their wedding masque, with its Utopian vision of love conquering all, was but a brief if pleasant fiction, they come to the end of themselves and the beginning of the knowledge of God. For the moment at least, they experience something deeper and stranger than anxiety. It is too resigned to be happiness; but it is a kind of peace.

AUDEN UNDERSTOOD, profoundly, that literary forms are ways of discerning the world: each of them reveals some aspect of experience while concealing others. (Things can be said in the epic that cannot be said in satire, and comedy discerns truths to which tragedy is blind.) It is for this reason that his longer poems display an almost encyclopedic variety of poetic forms and genres, none more so than *The Age of Anxiety*. We get a warning of what is to come in the poem's subtitle: "A Baroque Eclogue." The eclogue is a classical form, associated since Virgil with the meditations of shepherds—usually in groups. (The Zohar is actually an odd kind of eclogue, with rabbis rather than shepherds: the characters drift through Israel, pausing to rest under trees so they can converse about matters divine, in almost exactly the way that Arcadian shepherds lie about on hillsides contemplating the beauty of local shepherdesses.) This setting means that the eclogue is also a bucolic form, which makes it odd that it should be attached to a poem that begins and ends in New York City; but given the unpopulated visionary landscapes the characters move through, we cannot think the description merely ironic.

Auden calls the poem a *baroque* eclogue, and that is still more curious, given the elaborate ornamentation we associate with that tradition: it offers anything but the simplicity and cleanness of line we associate with the "classical." Yet the description is apt: the verse of *The Age of Anxiety* is nothing if not ornamented, and the poet seems to take joy in the ornamenting. (Auden once wrote that one of his tests of a critic's good taste was a genuine liking for "conscious theatrical exaggeration, pieces of Baroque flattery like Dryden's welcome to the Duchess of Ormond.")

But this is just the beginning of complications. The primary verse form of the poem is a four-beat line, with three alliterations per line. *Beowulf* is often mentioned in descriptions of this verse, but the form preceded *Beowulf* in Anglo-Saxon verse and would last hundreds of years afterward. (Its last great master was the anonymous author of *Sir Gawain and the Green Knight* and other poems, who was probably a contemporary of Chaucer. Indeed, *Sir Gawain*, with its passage through symbolic landscapes and its scenes of temptation, is one of the works that most powerfully underlies *The Age of Anxiety*. Auden himself associated the versification with another great medieval poem, *Piers Plowman*.) The poem contains several lyrics that draw on other medieval forms, including some from Old Norse, a language in which he was deeply interested. But the reader is just as likely to come across parodies or pastiches of the novelty songs that the jukeboxes and radios of the 1940s offered in large doses. (Auden complained to Alan Ansen about the impossibility of escaping them, in the diners of Swarthmore as much as in the dives of Manhattan.)

So, just as we find a rich thematic layering in this poem—concepts from the Zohar overlapping with the *paysage moralisé* tradition, and all bonded to a dream-quest—we see a similar layering of technical elements from the ancient world, the Middle Ages, the early modern, and the utterly contemporary. To some extent these multiple variations are simply a function of Auden's technical brilliance and the delight he took in exhibiting it; but there are more important reasons for such overwhelming complexity. Chief among them is Auden's conviction, already noted, that "the great vice of our age . . . is that we are all not only 'actors' but know that we are." We are "reduplicated Hamlets" in that we are eternally and pathologically self-conscious— we are always, like Quant at the outset of the poem, peering into our mirrors. In the introduction to John Betjeman's verse mentioned earlier, Auden writes, "For better or worse, we who live in this age not only feel but are critically conscious of our emotions—there is no difference in this respect between the highest of highbrows and the most farouche of soda jerkers—and, in consequence, again for better or worse, a naïve rhetoric, one that is not confessedly 'theatrical,' is now impossible in poetry. The honest manly style is today only suited to Iago." With this point in mind, one understands better why Auden dedicated this poem to Betjeman.

In *The Age of Anxiety*, therefore, Auden forcibly explores the manifold varieties of artifice; he multiplies forms and genres dizzyingly. If "reduplicated Hamlets" prefer to discreetly observe themselves in an elegant pier glass, Auden offers instead a funhouse hall of mirrors. The counterpart to Quant's opening look at himself in the bar is this dark thought from Malin's concluding soliloquy: "one / Staggers to the bathroom and stares in the glass / To meet one's madness." (Hamlet again: "You go not till I set you up a glass / Where you may see the inmost part of you.") Images are repeatedly and variously warped; the characters grow disoriented, dizzy, and faint. In the midst of this constant change Rosetta and Malin find only one still point.

THE STRATEGY that Auden pursues here has its risks, and it is tempting simply to say that it didn't work. *The Age of Anxiety* is not widely read and has never been fully understood. A book with such complexly intertwining themes probably should not feature such complexly intertwining techniques—even (or especially) if one of its chief concerns is the danger of artificiality. One can sympathize with the reader who says to the poet, "Physician, heal thyself."

Moreover—and this is clearly a related point—the experiences of the characters here are abstract and intellectual to the highest degree. Less than a decade after writing this poem, Auden would write of Kierkegaard that "a planetary visitor might read through the whole of his voluminous works without discovering that human beings are not ghosts but have bodies of flesh and blood"—but one could almost say the same of the four characters of *The Age of Anxiety*. The body that has the greatest role in the poem is the symbolic one he borrowed from the Zohar and made more obscure. As Edward Mendelson has commented, "Auden's efforts to write a poetry of the body were frustrated by his insistence on writing about symbols of the body rather than the body itself."

This defect he would soon remedy: the poems he would produce in the next decade are constantly absorbed in contemplation of human embodiment. But *The Age of Anxiety* remains a vitally important poem—in some ways a great one. It is surely his most ambitious work: formidably complex as his previous two long poems are, their themes are more bounded. "For the Time Being" meditates on the entry of the Divine into history; "The Sea and the Mirror" on the relationship between art and religious belief. These are large concerns, to be sure, but delimited. The question of what makes for an age of anxiety, on the other hand, is vaster and more amorphous: the condition itself must be described, and its etiology traced. A common anxiety manifests itself differently in those with and without religion; and for both groups alike it is fed by political, social, familial, and personal disorders. In *The Age of Anxiety* Auden tries to account for all of these, and if he falls short, that is a necessary result of such comprehensive ambition.

The poem quickly captured the imagination of its cultural moment, and not just because its title provided a terse and widely applicable diagnostic phrase. Thanks in part to some glowing early reviews— the most notable of them being Jacques Barzun's commendation in *Harper's*—and a profile of the poet that appeared in *Time* magazine the week of the poem's publication, it was reprinted four times within two years of its first appearance. *The Age of Anxiety* received the Pulitzer Prize for poetry in 1948, and inspired Leonard Bernstein's Symphony no. 2 for Piano and Orchestra, *The Age of Anxiety* (1949)—an attempt to render the plot and tone of the poem in musical terms, without words. Jerome Robbins choreographed a ballet set to Bernstein's symphony (1950); Auden, who never cared for ballet, reportedly especially disliked this one.

A stage version of the poem was presented in New York by the Living Theater Studio in 1954, but Auden seems to have had no involvement in it. However, in 1960 an undergraduate group at Princeton, Theatre Intime, staged an abridged version of the poem, with narration played through a television on stage, and Auden was sufficiently pleased by this adaptation that he agreed to serve as one of those televised narrators. (In the printed program he is identified as "Communicator.") So the poem has proven capable of vivid re-presentation, in multiple forms and genres.

In 1953 Auden would write of the moment when, each morning, we emerge from our private worlds: "Now each of us / Prays to an image of his image of himself." *The Age of Anxiety* is an extraordinarily acute anatomy of our self-images, and a diagnosis of those images' power not just to shape but to create our ideas. And it contains some of Auden's most powerful and beautiful verse: the compressed lyric "Hushed is the lake of hawks," the great Dirge of Part Four, the twin final speeches of Rosetta and Malin. This poem, for all its strangeness and extravagant elaboration of theme and technique, deserves a central place in the canon of twentieth-century poetry.

THE TEXT

Several of Auden's surviving holograph notebooks contain drafts of *The Age of Anxiety*. A notebook in the Berg Collection of the New York Public Library contains drafts of just a few speeches, but far more extensive notebooks are held at the Harry Ransom Center at the University of Texas and Yale's Beinecke Library. Almost all of the material in these two notebooks comes from a very late stage in the compositional process: the speeches tend to be close to their published forms, in many cases identical. The first forty pages of the Ransom notebook have been torn out, which suggests that Auden may have destroyed earlier sketches and outlines; but in any case little earlier material survives.

Though the verse itself in these notebooks is highly polished, there are few indications of the structure that the poem would ultimately assume. The order of the speeches only occasionally anticipates that of the published poem—the very first entry in the Beinecke notebook is a version of Malin's concluding speech, which is followed by speeches from various parts of the poem—and only rarely are the speakers indicated. Moreover, when speakers are noted, usually initials only are provided, and variable ones at that: A, B, J, M. At one point in the Beinecke notebook a series of stanzas are labeled A B C D A B C D A, and in the margin A is identified as "Civ" (presumably Quant), B as "Doc" (Malin), C as "girl" (Rosetta), and D as "M.S." ("Merchant Seaman" Emble). The initials of the names Auden eventually settled on appear only toward the end of the Ransom notebook—the

one clear suggestion that it was used later than the one in the Bei-
necke. The only sign of the prose narration that would eventually pro-
vide interpretative context for the verse comes on the inside back
cover of the Beinecke notebook: a small passage from what would
become Part Four, though, interestingly, in verse: "some Gilgamesh or
Napoleon, / Some Solon or Sherlock Holmes."

During the years that Auden worked on this poem, a young Ameri-
can poet named Alan Ansen (1922–2006) was his unofficial secretary,
amanuensis, and would-be Boswell. Ansen—who after his time with
Auden would become the model for Rollo Greb in Jack Kerouac's *On
the Road*—kept careful track of Auden's opinions in a notebook, which
he published years later as *The Table Talk of W. H. Auden*, often cited in
the notes below; he likewise attended Auden's lectures on Shake-
speare at the New School and transcribed them as carefully and com-
pletely as he could. And, most important for our purposes here, he
assisted Auden in several ways during and after the publication of *The
Age of Anxiety*.

Ansen's most important service was to type for Auden the whole
poem. (The manuscript he worked from has not been found.) The
typescript, now in the Berg Collection of the New York Public Library
along with Ansen's other literary remains, is quite close to the version
that would be published by Random House in July 1947.

Ansen referred to the typescript as the "Isherwood text," because in
December of 1946 it was sent to Auden's friend Christopher Isher-
wood. It is not clear when or how Isherwood returned the typescript,
though the presence in the Berg of the original envelope (addressed
to Isherwood at his home in Santa Monica, California) suggests that
Isherwood simply brought it with him when he came to New York in
early 1947, or when he returned some months later. It does not ap-
pear that he made any comments on the typescript, and he may never
have read the poem. However, the pages bear a number of correc-
tions and annotations by Auden and Ansen, who evidently used it to
prepare the text for the publisher. Auden's marks usually correct

spelling errors that Ansen made as a result of misreading the poet's handwriting ("lovelies" for "lonelies," for instance, and "Abyssinia" for "Abyssus"); significant changes (described in the notes at the back of this edition) in Ansen's hand, though clearly made at Auden's direction, occur frequently.

Ansen was useful to Auden not just as a typist, but also as a polyglot whose linguistic knowledge the poet could draw upon, and—most important of all—as someone attentive to prosody. "I'm never going to be able to let you go," Ansen records Auden saying to him. "I've never met anyone outside yourself who makes any effort to count—to see what one's doing." And Ansen counted indeed: probably during the typing of Auden's manuscript he came to notice a number of lines that failed to follow the metrical rules Auden had set for himself, and began to keep track of them in a handful of typed documents with such titles as "The Age Of Anxiety: Prolegomena To An Apparatus Criticus" and "Syllabifications To Be Reconsidered For The English Edition Of The Age Of Anxiety" and "Some Further Notes On The Syllabification Of The Age Of Anxiety" and "Further Notes On Syllabification." He was extraordinarily thorough and spurred Auden on to his own corrections: these, handwritten on two pages, accompany Ansen's notes in the Berg Collection.

Ansen's comment that these notes are "To Be Reconsidered For The English Edition Of The Age Of Anxiety" suggests that they had been made too late for Random House's first American printing, on 11 July 1947, but as it turned out, the poem had a second impression in August, so the changes were made for that printing. (However, they were, inexplicably, not incorporated into Faber and Faber's first English edition when it finally appeared, more than a year later.)

The most frequent changes for the second impression involve the shifting of words from the beginning of one line to the end of the previous one: in the first edition he had generally avoided feminine endings and as a result had made the verse overly iambic. I have incorporated all those changes in the text of this edition and, except in the case of the tiniest adjustments of punctuation, have indicated the first impression's reading in the notes. (More about Auden's technical ambitions for the poem may be discerned in the two letters reprinted in the Appendix.)

The text presented here is nearly identical to the one that Edward Mendelson has provided in the *Collected Poems*. The chief differences occur in three speeches from Part Three that Auden later extracted from the poem and published as "Three Dreams," and even these variations are quite minor.

Ansen had another role in the preparation of this manuscript: Auden asked him to write a blurb for the dust jacket. This Ansen tried to do, but Auden was not satisfied with the result and wrote his own. The version that ultimately appeared was heavily edited—brief and almost cursory, but not without interest:

> Mr. Auden's latest poem, *The Age of Anxiety*, is an eclogue; that is to say, it adopts the pastoral convention in which a natural setting is contrasted with an artificial style of diction. The setting, in this case, is a bar on Third Avenue, New York City, later an apartment on the West Side, the time an All-Souls' Night during the late war. The characters, a woman and three men, two in uniform, speak in alliterative verse.

The version that Ansen typed up for Auden was far too long to be used—but far more interesting to the reader of the poem. Included here are phrases struck through on the typescript:

BLURB FOR THE AGE OF ANXIETY

W. H. Auden's latest poem opens in a Third Avenue bar, where ~~four people~~ a few stray customers have come to seek relief from the tensions of wartime New York. It is the evening of All Souls'

Day, ~~the day of prayer for spirits not yet worthy of the Beatific Vision~~ and the faithful are concluding their prayers for the spirits still engaged in the ambiguities of purgation.

Malin, the medical intelligence officer with his pride of intellect and forbidden affections, Emble, the young sailor who is too handsome for his own good, Rosetta, the shrewd department store buyer trying to build a factitious repose out of day-dreams and sexual adventures, and Quant, the middle-aged shipping clerk harassed by the monotony of his occupation and the indiscriminateness of his diversions—all four patently stand in need of like intercession.

The radio squawks its depressing news, and they draw together to consider first their immediate historical plight and then, under the guidance of Malin, the seven ages of man. Stimulated by liquor and dissatisfied with their analysis, they dream of a state of unhistorical happiness which, as it turns out, involves only continual temptation and perpetual disappointment.

FINAL PARAGRAPH A

At Rosetta's suggestion they adjourn to her apartment. There the crucial decisions of the evening are taken. ~~How the characters are helped to renounce what they obviously ought not to have, how lovers' meetings end in journeys~~ Help in arriving at correct ones is available, but its effect on the journeys in which lovers' meetings end the reader must find out for himself.

FINAL PARAGRAPH B

At Rosetta's suggestion they adjourn to her apartment. There the characters are helped to the crucial renunciations of the evening. The last two sections of the poem end with two great monologues, indices to that grasp of historical reality and insight into the human condition which make *The Age of Anxiety* a major contribution to American culture.

POSSIBLE ADDITIONAL PARAGRAPHS TO
FOLLOW FINAL PARAGRAPH A

The poet has rejected the troublesome and modern bondage of rhyming in favor of a return to Germanic alliterative metres, the metres of *Piers Ploughman* and the Skalds. He has tightened up Langland's line and indulged in bold experiments which will be of interest to all amateurs of the art.

In the course of the poem may be found definitive laments over the sufferings imposed by the late war on land, on the sea, in the air, and on the home front, the torch song to end all torch songs, and an elaborate dirge for a wartime leader. And the two great monologues which end the last two sections of the poem only epitomize that grasp of historical reality and insight into the human condition which make *The Age of Anxiety* a major contribution to American culture.

It might be appropriate here to cite the blurb written for the English edition—based on the final American version, but more praiseful in some ways while in others betraying some uncertainty about the poem's overall success—by Auden's editor at Faber, T. S. Eliot:

Mr. Auden's new long poem takes the form of a dialogue between a woman and three men: the place, first a bar on Third Avenue, second, an apartment on the West Side of New York; the time an All Souls' Night during the War. The content of the poem, like that of Mr. Auden's previous two volumes, will arouse endless discussion and argument; the form is one more illustration of the author's inexhaustible resourcefulness and mastery of versification, which become more astonishing with every work he puts forth.

FINALLY, SOMETHING needs to be said about the appearance of this edition. In January of 1947 Auden told Alan Ansen, "In my contract for *The Age of Anxiety*, I specified that I wanted to have control over the details of printing. . . . The book is going to be very small, the poetry is set in very small type and the prose still smaller." The current volume is not as small as the first American edition, and most later ones—they were only 4.75 by 7.5 inches—and the type is larger.

In other respects, the appearance of this edition differs from Auden's expressed wishes. He frequently quarreled with his American publisher, Random House, about the appearance of his books. "It isnt that I dont realise that, as such things go, the fount [font] is well designed," he wrote to Bennett Cerf in 1944. "It's a matter of principle. You would never think of using such a fount for, say, 'The Embryology of the Elasmobranch Liver', so why use it for poetry? I feel very strongly that 'aesthetic' books should not be put in a special class." And then, in 1951, he told *Publishers Weekly*, "I have a violent prejudice against arty paper and printing which is too often considered fitting for unsalable prestige books, and by inverted snobbery I favor the shiny white paper and format of the textbook. Further, perhaps because I am near-sighted and hold the page nearer my nose than is normal, I have a strong preference for small type."

During the preparations for the publication of *The Age of Anxiety*, Auden made sure that Random House understood his position. As Nicholas Jenkins explains,

> In 1946, when he told Random House what he wanted for *The Age of Anxiety*, he loaned them his copy of *A Treatise on a Section of the Strata from Newcastle-upon-Tyne to Cross Fell, with Remarks on Mineral Veins*, by Westgarth Forster, a book originally published in 1821 but that he seems to have owned in the third edition of 1883, and instructed them to copy its appearance. They did. *A Treatise on a Section of the Strata* had been set in Scotch, an extremely popular 19th century typeface, and the Kingsport Press

in Tennessee used the Linotype version of Scotch for Auden's book.

Though modern digital versions of Scotch exist, this volume uses the same basic typographic design used in earlier volumes in the W.H. Auden Critical Editions series and does not attempt to follow Auden's specifications for the 1947 edition. The sharp, consistent digital fonts used in the early twenty-first century cannot accurately reproduce the irregular, rough-edged, hot-metal typography produced by a Linotype machine in 1947, and any attempt to do so would produce an unpleasant example of typographic kitsch. A representative page of the original is reproduced on the facing page and may give some sense of the typographic flavor that Auden wanted.

Now   The ground's aggression is growing less.
ROSETTA
says: The clouds are clearing.

EMBLE   My cape is dry.
says:
    I can reckon correctly.

MALIN   My real intentions
says:
    Are nicer now.

And   I'm nearing the top.
QUANT
says: When I hear what I'm up to, how I shall laugh.

And so, on a treeless watershed, at the tumbledown Mariners Tavern (which is miles inland) the four assemble, having completed the first stage of their journey. They look about them, and everything seems somehow familiar. Emble says:

> The railroads like the rivers run for the most
> > part
> > East and west, and from here
> On a clear day both coasts are visible
> > And the long piers of their ports.
> To the south one sees the sawtooth range
> > Our nickel and copper come from,
> And beyond it the Barrens used for Army
> > Manœuvres; while to the north

66

THE AGE OF ANXIETY

A Baroque Eclogue

Lacrimosa dies illa
Qua resurget ex favilla
Iudicandus homo reus

THOMAS A CELANO (?)
Dies Irae

TO JOHN BETJEMAN

PART ONE

Prologue

Now the day is over,
Night is drawing nigh,
Shadows of the evening
Steal across the sky.

S. BARING-GOULD

When the historical process breaks down and armies organize with their embossed debates the ensuing void which they can never consecrate, when necessity is associated with horror and freedom with boredom, then it looks good to the bar business.

In times of peace there are always a number of persons who wake up each morning excited by the prospect of another day of interesting and difficult work, or happily certain that the one with whom they shared their bed last night will be sharing it with them again the next, and who, in consequence, must be written off by the proprietor as a lost market. Not that he need worry. There will always be enough lonelies and enough failures who need desperately what he has to offer—namely, an unprejudiced space in which nothing particular ever happens, and a choice of physiological aids to the imagination whereby each may appropriate it for his or her private world of repentant felicitous forms, heavy expensive objects or avenging flames and floods—to guarantee him a handsome profit still.

But in war-time, when everybody is reduced to the anxious status of a shady character or a displaced person, when even the most prudent become worshippers of chance, and when, in comparison to the universal disorder of the world outside, his Bohemia seems as cosy and respectable as a suburban villa, he can count on making his fortune.

Looking up from his drink, QUANT caught the familiar eye of his reflection in the mirror behind the bar and wondered why he was still so interested in that tired old widower who would never be more now than a clerk in a shipping office near the Battery.

More, that is, as a public figure: for as so often happens in the modern world—and how much restlessness, envy and self-contempt it causes—there was no one-to-one correspondence between his social or economic position and his private mental life. He had come to America at the age of six when his father, implicated somehow in the shooting of a landlord, had had to leave Ireland in a hurry, and, from time to time, images, some highly-colored, some violent, derived from a life he could not remember, would enter unexpectedly and incomprehensibly into his dreams. Then, again, in early manhood, when unemployed during a depression, he had spent many hours one winter in the Public Library reading for the most part—he could not have told you why—books on Mythology. The knowledge gained at that time had ever since lain oddly around in a corner of his mind like luggage left long ago in an emergency by some acquaintance and never reclaimed.

Watching the bubbles rise in his glass, MALIN was glad to forget for his few days of leave the uniform of the Canadian Air Force he was wearing and the life it represented, at once disjointed and mechanical, alternately exhausting and idle, of a Medical Intelligence officer; trying to recapture the old atmosphere of laboratory and lecture hall, he returned with pleasure to his real interests.

Lighting a cigarette, ROSETTA, too, ignored her surroundings but with less ease. Yes, she made lots of money—she was a buyer for a big department store and did it very well—and that was a great deal, for, like anyone who has ever been so, she had a sensible horror of being poor. Yes, America was the best place on earth to come to if you had to earn your living, but did it have to be so big and empty and noisy and messy? Why could she not have been rich? Yes, though she was

not as young as she looked, there were plenty of men who either were
deceived or preferred a girl who might be experienced—which in-
deed she was. But why were the men one liked not the sort who pro-
posed marriage and the men who proposed marriage not the sort one
liked? So she returned now to her favorite day-dream in which she
indulged whenever she got a little high—which was rather too often—
and conjured up, detail by detail, one of those landscapes familiar to
all readers of English detective stories, those lovely innocent country-
sides inhabited by charming eccentrics with independent means and
amusing hobbies to whom, until the sudden intrusion of a horrid
corpse onto the tennis court or into the greenhouse, work and law
and guilt are just literary words.

EMBLE, on the other hand, put down his empty glass and looked
about him as if he hoped to read in all those faces the answer to his
own disquiet. Having enlisted in the Navy during his sophomore year
at a Mid-Western university, he suffered from that anxiety about him-
self and his future which haunts, like a bad smell, the minds of most
young men, though most of them are under the illusion that their
lack of confidence is a unique and shameful fear which, if confessed,
would make them an object of derision to their normal contempo-
raries. Accordingly, they watch others with a covert but passionate
curiosity. What makes them tick? What would it feel like to be a suc-
cess? Here is someone who is nobody in particular, there even an obvi-
ous failure, yet they do not seem to mind. How is that possible? What
is their secret?

In certain cases—his was one—this general unease of youth is only
aggravated by what would appear to alleviate it, a grace of person
which grants them, without effort on their part, a succession of sexual
triumphs. For then the longing for success, the doubt of ever being
able to achieve the kinds of success which have to be earned, and the
certainty of being able to have at this moment a kind which does not,
play dangerously into each other's hands.

So, fully conscious of the attraction of his uniform to both sexes, he looked round him, slightly contemptuous when he caught an admiring glance, and slightly piqued when he did not.

It was the night of All Souls.

QUANT was thinking:

My deuce, my double, my dear image,
Is it lively there, that land of glass
Where song is a grimace, sound logic
A suite of gestures? You seem amused.
How well and witty when you wake up,
How glad and good when you go to bed,
Do you feel, my friend? What flavor has
That liquor you lift with your left hand;
Is it cold by contrast, cool as this
For a soiled soul; does your self like mine
Taste of untruth? Tell me, what are you
Hiding in your heart, some angel face,
Some shadowy she who shares in my absence,
Enjoys my jokes? I'm jealous, surely,
Nicer myself (though not as honest),
The marked man of romantic thrillers
Whose brow bears the brand of a winter
No priest can explain, the poet disguised,
Thinking over things in thieves' kitchens,
Wanted by the waste, whom women's love
Or his own silhouette might all too soon
Betray to its tortures. I'll track you down,
I'll make you confess how much you know who
View my vices with a valet's slight
But shameless shrug, the *Schadenfreude*
Of cooks at keyholes. Old comrade, tell me
The lie of my lifetime but look me up in
Your good graces; agree to be friends

Till our deaths differ; drink, strange future,
To your neighbor now.

MALIN was thinking:

                No chimpanzee
Thinks it thinks. Things are divisible,
Creatures are not. In chaos all bodies
Would differ in weight. Dogs can learn to
Fear the future. The faceless machine
Lacks a surround. The laws of science have
Never explained why novelty always
Arrives to enrich (though the wrong question
Imitates nothing). Nature rewards
Perilous leaps. The prudent atom
Simply insists upon its safety now,
Security at all costs; the calm plant
Masters matter then submits to itself,
Busy but not brave; the beast assures
A stabler status to stolen flesh,
Assists though it enslaves: singular then
Is the human way; for the ego is a dream
Till a neighbor's need by name create it;
Man has no mean; his mirrors distort;
His greenest arcadias have ghosts too;
His utopias tempt to eternal youth
Or self-slaughter.

ROSETTA was thinking:

              From Seager's Folly
We beheld what was ours. Undulant land
Rose layer by later till at last the sea
Far away flashed; from fretted uplands
That lay to the north, from limestone heights
Incisive rains had dissected well,

For down each dale industrious there ran
A paternoster of ponds and mills,
Came sweet waters, assembling quietly
By a clear congress of accordant streams
A mild river that moseyed at will
Through parks and ploughland, purring southward
In a wide valley. Wolds on each side
Came dawdling downwards in double curves,
Mellow, mature, to meadowlands and
Sedentary orchards, settled places
Crowded with lives; fat cattle brooded
In the shade of great oaks, sheep grazed in
The ancient hollows of meander scars and
Long-legged ladies with little-legged dogs
Lolled with their lovers by lapsing brooks.
A couth region: consonant, lofty,
Volatile vault and vagrant buttress
Showed their shapeliness; with assured ease,
Proud on that plain, St Peter Acorn,
St Dill-in-the-Deep, St Dust, St Alb,
St Bee-le-bone, St Botolph-the-less,
High gothic growths in a grecian space,
Lorded over each leafy parish
Where country curates in cold bedrooms
Dreamed of deaneries till at day-break
The rector's rooks with relish described
Their stinted station.

EMBLE was thinking:
                Estranged, aloof,
They brood over being till the bars close,
The malcontented who might have been
The creative odd ones the average need

To suggest new goals. Self-judged they sit,
Sad haunters of Perhaps who after years
To grasp and gaze in get no further
Than their first beholding, phantoms who try
Through much drink by magic to restore
The primitive pact with pure feeling,
Their flesh as it felt before sex was
(The archaic calm without cultural sin
Which her Adam is till his Eve does),
Eyeing the door, for ever expecting
Night after night the Nameless One, the
Smiling sea-god who shall safely land
Shy and broad-shouldered on the shore at last,
Enthusiastic, of their convenient
And dangerous dream; while days away, in
Prairie places where no person asks
What is suffered in ships, small tradesmen,
Wry relatives on rocking-chairs in
Moss-grown mansions, mothers whose causes
For right and wrong are unreal to them,
Grieve vaguely over theirs: their vision shrinks
As their dreams darken; with dulling voice
Each calls across a colder water,
Tense, optative, interrogating
Some sighing several who sadly fades.

But now the radio, suddenly breaking in with its banal noises upon their separate senses of themselves, by compelling them to pay attention to a common world of great slaughter and much sorrow, began, without their knowledge, to draw these four strangers closer to each other. For in response to its official doctored message:

> *Now the news. Night raids on*
> *Five cities. Fires started.*

Pressure applied by pincer movement
In threatening thrust. Third Division
Enlarges beachhead. Lucky charm
Saves sniper. Sabotage hinted
In steel-mill stoppage. Strong point held
By fanatical Nazis. Canal crossed
By heroic marines. Rochester barber
Fools foe. Finns ignore
Peace feeler. Pope condemns
Axis excesses. Underground
Blows up bridge. Thibetan prayer-wheels
Revolve for victory. Vital crossroads
Taken by tanks. Trend to the left
Forecast by Congressman. Cruiser sunk
In Valdivian Deep. Doomed sailors
Play poker. Reporter killed.

MALIN thought:

Untalkative and tense, we took off
Anxious into air; our instruments glowed,
Dials in darkness, for dawn was not yet;
Pulses pounded; we approached our target,
Conscious in common of our closed Here
And of Them out There, thinking of Us
In a different dream, for we die in theirs
Who kill in ours and become fathers,
Not twisting tracks their trigger hands are
Given goals by; we began our run;
Death and damage darted at our will,
Bullets were about, blazing anger
Lunged from below, but we had laid our eggs
Neatly in their nest, a nice deposit,
Hatched in an instant; houses flamed in

Shuddering sheets as we shed our big
Tears on their town: we turned to come back,
But at high altitudes, hostile brains
Waited in the west, a wily flock
Vowed to vengeance in the vast morning,
—A mild morning where no marriage was,
And gravity a god greater than love—
Fierce interferers. We fought them off
But paid a price; there was pain for some.
"Why have They killed me?" wondered our Bert, our
Greenhouse gunner, forgot our answer,
Then was not with us. We watched others
Drop into death; dully we mourned each
Flare as it fell with a friend's lifetime,
While we hurried on to our home bases
To the safe smells and a sacrament
Of tea with toast. At twenty to eight I
Stepped onto grass, still with the living,
While far and near a fioritura
Of brooks and blackbirds bravely struck the
International note with no sense
Of historic truth, of time meaning
Once and for all, and my watch stuttered:—
Many have perished; more will.

And QUANT thought:

All war's woes I can well imagine.
Gun-barrels glint, gathered in ambush,
Mayhem among mountains; minerals break
In by order on intimate groups of
Tender tissues; at their tough visit
Flesh flusters that was so fluent till now,
Stammers some nonsense, stops and sits down,

Apathetic to all this. Thousands lie in
Ruins by roads, irrational in woods,
Insensitive upon snow-bound plains,
Or littered lifeless along low coasts
Where shingle shuffles as shambling waves
Feebly fiddle in the fading light
With bloated bodies, beached among groynes,
Male no longer, unmotivated,
Have-beens without hopes: Earth takes charge of,
Soil accepts for a serious purpose
The jettisoned blood of jokes and dreams,
Making buds from bone, from brains the good
Vague vegetable; survivors play
Cards in kitchens while candles flicker
And in blood-spattered barns bandaged men,
Their poor hands in a panic of need
Groping weakly for a gun-butt or
A friendly fist, are fetched off darkling.
Many have perished; more will.

And EMBLE thought:
High were those headlands; the eagles promised
Life without lawyers. Our long convoy
Turned away northward as tireless gulls
Wove over water webs of brightness
And sad sound. The insensible ocean,
Miles without mind, moaned all around our
Limited laughter, and below our songs
Were deaf deeps, denes of unaffection,
Their chill unchanging, chines where only
The whale is warm, their wildness haunted
By metal fauna moved by reason
To hunt not in hunger but for hate's sake,

Stalking our steamers. Strained with gazing
Our eyes ached, and our ears as we slept
Kept their care for the crash that would turn
Our fears into fact. In the fourth watch
A torpedo struck on the port bow:
The blast killed many; the burning oil
Suffocated some; some in lifebelts
Floated upright till they froze to death;
The younger swam but the yielding waves
Denied help; they were not supported,
They swallowed and sank, ceased thereafter
To appear in public; exposed to snap
Verdicts of sharks, to vague inquiries
Of amoeboid monsters, mobbed by slight
Unfriendly fry, refused persistence.
They are nothing now but names assigned to
Anguish in others, areas of grief.
Many have perished; more will.

ROSETTA thought:

I see in my mind a besieged island,
That island in arms where my home once was.
Round green gardens, down grooves between white
Hawthorn-hedges, long hospital trains
Smoothly slide with their sensitized freight
Of mangled men, moving them homeward
In pain through pastures. In a packed hall
Two vicious rivals, two virtuosos
Appear on one platform and play duets
To war-orphans and widowed ladies,
Grieving in gloves; while to grosser ears
In clubs and cabarets crooners wail
Some *miserere* modern enough

In its thorough thinness. I think too of
The conquered condition, countries where
Arrogant officers, armed in cars,
Go roaring down roads on the wrong side,
Courts martial meet at midnight with drums,
And pudgy persons pace unsmiling
The quays and stations or cruise the nights
In vans for victims, to investigate
In sound-proof cells the Sense of Honor,
While in turkish baths with towels round them
Imperilled plotters plan in outline
Definitions and norms for new lives,
Half-truths for their times. As tense as these,
Four who are famous confer in a *schloss*
At night on nations. They are not equal:
Three stand thoughtful on a thick carpet
Awaiting the Fourth who wills they shall
Till, suddenly entering through a side-door,
Quick, quiet, unquestionable as death,
Grief or guilt, he greets them and sits down,
Lord of this life. He looks natural,
He smiles well, he smells of the future,
Odorless ages, an ordered world
Of planned pleasures and passport-control,
Sentry-go, sedatives, soft drinks and
Managed money, a moral planet
Tamed by terror: his telegram sets
Grey masses moving as the mud dries.
Many have perished; more will.

And when in conclusion the instrument said:

> *Buy a bond. Blood saves lives.*
> *Donate now. Name this station.*

they could no longer keep these thoughts to themselves, but turning
towards each other on their high wooden stools, became acquainted.

ROSETTA spoke first:

    Numbers and nightmares have news value.

Then MALIN:

    A crime has occurred, accusing all.

Then QUANT:

    The world needs a wash and a week's rest.

To which EMBLE said:

    Better this than barbarian misrule.
    History tells more often than not
    Of wickedness with will, wisdom but
    An interjection without a verb,
    And the godless growing like green cedars
    On righteous ruins. The reticent earth,
    Exposed by the spade, speaks its warning
    With successive layers of sacked temples
    And dead civilians. They dwelt at ease
    In their sown centers, sunny their minds,
    Fine their features; their flesh was carried
    On beautiful bones; they bore themselves
    Lightly through life; they loved their children
    And entertained with all their senses
    A world of detail. Wave and pebble,
    Boar and butterfly, birch and carp, they
    Painted as persons, portraits that seem
    Neighbors with names; one knows from them what
    A leaf must feel. By lakes at twilight
    They sang of swans and separations,
    Mild, unmilitant, as the moon rose

And reeds rustled; ritual appointed
Tastes and textures; their touch preferred the
Spectrum of scents to Spartan morals,
Art to action. But, unexpected, as
Bells babbled in a blossoming month,
Near-sighted scholars on canal paths
Defined their terms, and fans made public
The hopes of young hearts, out of the north, from
Black tundras, from basalt and lichen,
Peripheral people, rancid ones
Stocky on horses, stomachs in need of
Game and grazing, by grass corridors
Coursed down on their concatenation
Of smiling cities. Swords and arrows
Accosted their calm; their climate knew
Fire and fear; they fell, they bled, not an
Eye was left open; all disappeared:
Utter oblivion they had after that.

MALIN said:

But the new barbarian is no uncouth
Desert-dweller; he does not emerge
From fir forests; factories bred him;
Corporate companies, college towns
Mothered his mind, and many journals
Backed his beliefs. He was born here. The
Bravura of revolvers in vogue now
And the cult of death are quite at home
Inside the city.

QUANT said:

The soldiers' fear
And the shots will cease in a short while,
More ruined regions surrender to less,

Prominent persons be put to death
For mass-murder, and what moves us now,
The defence of friends against foes' hate,
Be over for ever. Then, after that,
What shall we will? Why shall we practise
Vice or virtue when victory comes?
The celebrations are suddenly hushed,
The coarse crowds are uncomfortably still,
For, arm-in-arm now, behind the festooned
Conqueror's car there come his heirs, the
Public hangman, the private wastrel.

ROSETTA said:
Lies and lethargies police the world
In its periods of peace. What pain taught
Is soon forgotten; we celebrate
What ought to happen as if it were done,
Are blinded by our boasts. Then back they come,
The fears that we fear. We fall asleep
Only to meet the idiot children of
Our revels and wrongs; farouche they appear,
Reluctant look-behinds, loitering through
The mooing gate, menacing or smiling,
Nocturnal trivia, torts and dramas,
Wrecks, arrivals, rose-bushes, armies,
Leopards and laughs, alarming growths of
Moulds and monsters on memories stuffed
With dead men's doodles, dossiers written
In lost lingos, too long an account
To take out in trade, no time either,
Since we wake up. We are warm, our active
Universe is young; yet we shiver:
For athwart our thinking the threat looms.
Huge and awful as the hump of Saturn

Over modest Mimas, of more deaths
And worse wars, a winter of distaste
To last a lifetime. Our lips are dry, our
Knees numb; the enormous disappointment
With a smiling sigh softly flings her
Indolent apron over our lives
And sits down on our day. Damning us,
On our present purpose the past weighs
Heavy as alps, for the absent are never
Mislaid or lost: as lawyers define
The grammar of our grief, their ghosts rise,
Hanged or headless, hosts who disputed
With good governors, their guilty flesh
Racked and raving but unreconciled,
The punished people to pass sentence
On the jolly and just; and, joining these
Come worse warlocks, the wailing infants
Who know now they will never be born,
Refused a future. Our failings give
Their resentment seizin; our Zion is
A doomed Sodom dancing its heart out
To treacly tunes, a tired Gomorrah
Infatuated with her former self
Whose dear dreams though they dominate still
Are formal faces which refresh no more.

They fell silent and immediately became conscious again of the
radio, now blandly inexorably bringing to all John Doakes and G.I.
Joes tidings of great joy and saying

> *Definitely different. Has that democratic*
> *Extra elegance. Easy to clean.*
> *Will gladden grand-dad and your girl friend.*
> *Lasts a lifetime. Leaves no odor.*

American made. A modern product
Of nerve and know-how with a new thrill.
Patriotic to own. Is on its way
In a patent package. Pays to investigate.
Serves through science. Has something added
By skilled Scotchmen. Exclusively used
By upper classmen and Uncle Sam.
Tops in tests by teenagers.
Just ask for it always.

Matter and manner set their teeth on edge, especially MALIN's
who felt like talking. So he ordered a round of drinks, then said:

Here we sit
Our bodies bound to these bar-room lights,
The night's odors, the noise of the El on
Third Avenue, but our thoughts are free...
Where shall they wander? To the wild past
When, beaten back, banished to their cirques
The horse-shoe glaciers curled up and died,
And cold-blooded through conifers slouched
Fumbling amphibians; forward into
Tidy utopias of eternal spring,
Vitamins, villas, visas for dogs
And art for all; or up and down through
Those hidden worlds of alien sizes
Which lenses elicit?

But EMBLE objected:
Muster no monsters, I'll meeken my own.

So did ROSETTA:
You may wish till you waste, I'll want here.

So did QUANT:

> Too blank the blink of these blind heavens.

MALIN suggested:

Let us then

> Consider rather the incessant Now of
> The traveler through time, his tired mind
> Biased towards bigness since his body must
> Exaggerate to exist, possessed by hope,
> Acquisitive, in quest of his own
> Absconded self yet scared to find it
> As he bumbles by from birth to death
> Menaced by madness; whose mode of being,
> Bashful or braggart, is to be at once
> Outside and inside his own demand
> For personal pattern. His pure I
> Must give account of and greet his Me,
> That field of force where he feels he thinks,
> His past present, presupposing death,
> Must ask what he is in order to be
> And make meaning by omission and stress,
> Avid of elseness. All that exists
> Matters to man; he minds what happens
> And feels he is at fault, a fallen soul
> With power to place, to explain every
> What in his world but why he is neither
> God nor good, this guilt the insoluble
> Final fact, infusing his private
> Nexus of needs, his noted aims with
> Incomprehensible comprehensive dread
> At not being what he knows that before
> This world was he was willed to become.

QUANT approved:

> Set him to song, the surly old dodger.

So did EMBLE:

> Relate his lies to his longings for truth.

So did ROSETTA:

> Question his crimes till his clues confess.

The radio attempted to interrupt by remarking

> *And now Captain Kidd in his Quiz Program*
> *HOW ALERT ARE YOU*

But QUANT pointed a finger at it and it stopped immediately. He said:

> Listen, Box,
> And keep quiet. Listen courteously to us
> Four reformers who have founded—why not?—
> The Gung-Ho Group, the Ganymede Club
> For homesick young angels, the Arctic League
> Of Tropical Fish, the Tomboy Fund
> For Blushing Brides and the Bide-a-wees
> Of Sans-Souci, assembled again
> For a Think-Fest: Our theme tonight is

> *HOMO ABYSSUS OCCIDENTALIS*
> *or*
> *A CURIOUS CASE OF COLD FEET*
> *or*
> *SEVEN SELFISH SUPPERLESS AGES*

And now, at ROSETTA's suggestion, they left their bar-stools and moved to the quieter intimacy of a booth. Drinks were ordered and the discussion began.

PART TWO

The Seven Ages

A sick toss'd vessel, dashing on each thing;
Nay, his own shelf:
My God, I mean myself.

GEORGE HERBERT *Miserie*

MALIN began:

Behold the infant, helpless in cradle and
Righteous still, yet already there is
Dread in his dreams at the deed of which
He knows nothing but knows he can do,
The gulf before him with guilt beyond,
Whatever that is, whatever why
Forbids his bound; till that ban tempts him;
He jumps and is judged: he joins mankind,
The fallen families, freedom lost,
Love become Law. Now he looks at grown-ups
With conscious care, and calculates on
The effect of a frown or filial smile,
Accuses with a cough, claims pity
With scratched knees, skillfully avenges
Pains and punishments on puny insects,
Grows into a grin, and gladly shares his
Small secret with the supplicating
Instant present. His emptiness finds
Its joy in a gang and is joined to others
By crimes in common. Clumsy and alarmed,
As the blind bat obeys the warnings

Of its own echoes, his inner life
Is a zig-zag, a bizarre dance of
Feelings through facts, a foiled one learning
Shyness and shame, a shadowed flier.

QUANT said:

                              O
Secret meetings at the slaughter-house
With nickels and knives, initiations
Behind the billboards. Then the hammerpond looked
So green and grim, yet graciously its dank
Water made us welcome—once in, we
Swam without swearing. The smelting mill
We broke into had a big chimney
And huge engines; holding our breath, we
Lighted matches and looked at the gears,
The cruel cogwheels, the crank's absolute
Veto on pleasure. In a vacant lot
We built a bonfire and burned alive
Some stolen tires. How strong and good one
Felt at first, how fagged coming home through
The urban evening. Heavy like us
Sank the gas-tanks—it was supper time.
In hot houses helpless babies and
Telephones gabbled untidy cries,
And on embankments black with burnt grass
Shambling freight-trains were shunted away
Past crimson clouds.

EMBLE said:

                     My cousins were both
Strong and stupid: they stole my candy,
They tied me to a tree, they twisted my arms,

Called me crybaby. "Take care," I sobbed,
I could hold up my hand and hot water
Would come down on your drought and drown you all
In your big boots." In our back garden
One dark afternoon I dug quite a hole
Planning to vanish.

ROSETTA said:
                    On picnic days
My dearest doll was deaf and spoke in
Grunts like grandfather. God understood
If we washed our necks he wasn't ever
To look in the loft where the Lamps were
And the Holy Hook. In the housekeeper's room there
Was currant cake and calves-foot jelly
As we did our sums while down below,
Tall in tweeds on the terrace gravel,
Father and his friends reformed régimes,
Monies and monarchs, and mother wrote
Swift and sure in the silk-hung saloon
Her large round letters. Along the esker,
Following a fox with our fingers crossed
Or after the ogre in Indian file,
We stole with our sticks through a still world of
Hilarious light, our lives united
Like fruit in a bowl, befriended by
The supple silence, incited by
Our shortened shadows.

MALIN went on to the Second Age:
                         With shaving comes
An hour when he halts, hearing the crescent
Roar of hazard, and realizes first

He has laid his life-bet with a lying self
Who wins or welches. Thus woken, he is
Amused no more by a merely given
Felt fact, the facile emergence of
Thought with thing, but, threatened from all sides,
Embarrassed by his body's bald statements,
His sacred soul obscenely tickled
And bellowed at by a blatant Without,
A dog by daylight, in dreams a lamb
Whom the nightmare ejects nude into
A ball of princes too big to feel
Disturbed by his distress, he starts off now,
Poor, unprepared, on his pilgrimage
To find his friends, the far-off *élite*,
And, knowing no one, a nameless young man,
Pictures as he plods his promised chair
In their small circle secret to those
With no analogies, unique persons,
The originals' ring, the round table
Of master minds. Mountains he loves now,
Piers and promontories, places where
Evening brings him all that grandeur
Of scope and scale which the sky is believed
To promise or recall, pacing by
In a sunset trance of self-pity,
While his toy tears with a touching grace
Like little balloons sail lonely away
To dusk and death.

QUANT said:

                    With diamonds to offer,
A cleaned tycoon in a cooled office,
I smiled at a siren with six breasts,
Leaning on leather, looking up at

Her righteous robber, her Robin Hood,
Her plump prince. All the public could see
Was a bus-boy brushing a table,
Sullen and slight.

ROSETTA said:

In my sixteenth year
Before sleeping I fancied nightly
The house on the headland I would own one day.
Its long windows overlooked the sea
And its turf terrace topped a sunny
Sequestered cove. A corkscrew staircase
From a green gate in the garden wall
Descended the cliff, the sole entrance
To my beach where bathers basked beside
The watchet waves. Though One was special,
All forms were friends who freely told their
Secrets to me; but, safe in my purse
I kept the key to the closet where
A sliding panel concealed the lift,
Known to none, which at night would take me
Down through the dark to my dock below,
A chamber chiselled in the chalk hill,
Private and perfect; thence, putting forth
Alone in my launch through a low tunnel
Out to the ocean, while all others slept,
Smiling and singing I sailed till dawn,
Happy, hatless.

EMBLE said:

After a dreadful
Row with father, I ran with burning
Cheeks to the pasture and chopped wood, my
Stomach like a stone. I strode that night

Through wicked dreams: waking, I skipped to
The shower and sang, ashamed to recall
With whom or how; the hiss of the water
Composed the tune, I supplied the words
For a fine dirge which fifty years hence
Massed choirs would sing as my coffin passed,
Grieved for and great on a gun-carriage.

MALIN went on, spoke of the Third Age:
Such pictures fade as his path is blocked
By Others from Elsewhere, alien bodies
Whose figures fasten on his free thoughts,
Ciphers and symbols secret to his flesh,
Uniquely near, needing his torments,
His lonely life, and he learns what real
Images are; that, however violent
Their wish to be one, that wild promise
Cannot be kept, their case is double;
For each now of need ignores the other as
By rival routes of recognition
Diminutive names that midnight hears
Intersect upon their instant way
To solid solitudes, and selves cross
Back to bodies, both insisting each
Proximate place a pertinent thing.
So, learning to love, at length he is taught
To know he does not.

QUANT said:
                    Since the neighbors did,
With a multitude I made the long
Visitors' voyage to Venus Island,

Elated as they, landed upon
The savage shore where old swains lay wrecked
Unfit for her fable, followed up
The basalt stairway bandying jokes with
The thoughtless throng, but then, avoiding
The great gate where she gives all pilgrims
Her local wine, I legged it over
A concrete wall, was cold sober as,
Pushing through brambles, I peeked out at
Her fascination. Frogs were shooting
Craps in a corner; cupids on stilts,
Their beautiful bottoms breaking wind,
Hunted hares with hurricane lanterns
Through woods on one side, while on the other,
Shining out through shivering poplars,
Stood a brick bath-house where burghers mixed
With light-fingered ladies and louche trade,
Dancing in serpents and daisy chains
To mad music. In the mid-distance
On deal chairs sat a dozen decayed
Gentlewomen with dejected backs
And raw fingers morosely stitching
Red flannel scivvies for heroic herms.
Primroses, peacocks and peachtrees made
A fair foreground but fairer there, with
An early Madonna's oval face
And lissom limbs, delighting that whole
Degraded glen, the Goddess herself
Presided smiling; a saucy wind,
Plucking from her thigh her pink wrapper
Of crêpe-de-chine, disclosed a very
Indolent ulcer.

ROSETTA said nothing but, placing a nickel in the Wallomatic, se-
lected a sad little tune *The Case Is Closed (Tchaikovsky-Fink)* and sang to it
softly:

> Deep in my dark the dream shines
> Yes, of you, you dear always;
> My cause to cry, cold but my
> Story still, still my music.
>
> Mild rose the moon, moving through our
> Naked nights: tonight it rains;
> Black umbrellas blossom out;
> Gone the gold, my golden ball.
>
> Heavy these hands. I believed
> That pleased pause, your pause was me
> To love alone till life's end:
> I thought this; this was not true.
>
> You touched, you took. Tears fall. O
> Fair my far, when far ago
> Like waterwheels wishes spun
> Radiant robes: but the robes tore.

EMBLE did likewise but his choice was a hot number, *Bugs in the Bed*
by *Bog Myrtle & Her Two-Timers.* He sang gaily:

> His Queen was forward, Her King was shy;
> He hoped for Her Heart but He overbid;
> When She ducked His Diamond down They went.
>
> In Smuggler's Cove He smelt near Him
> Her musical mermaids; She met His angels
> In Locksmith's Lane, the little dears.

He said to Her: "You're a hazy truth;"
She said to Him: "You're a shining lie;"
Each went to a washroom and wept much.

The public applauded and the poets drew
A moral for marriage: "The moths will get you
If the wolves won't, so why not now?"

The consequence was Both claimed the insurance
And the furniture gave what-for to Their elbows.
A reason for One, a risk on the Pair.

MALIN went on, spoke of the Fourth Age:
Now unreckoned with, rough, his road descends
From the haughty and high, the humorless places
His dreams would prefer, and drops him till,
As his forefathers did, he finds out
Where his world lies. By the water's edge,
The unthinking flood, down there, yes, is his
Proper place, the polychrome Oval
With its kleig lights and crowd engineers,
The mutable circus where mobs rule
The arena with roars, the real world of
Theology and horses, our home because
In that doubt-condemning dual kingdom
Signs and insignia decide our cause,
Fanatics of the Egg or Knights sworn to
Die for the Dolphin, and our deeds wear
Heretic green or orthodox blue,
Safe and certain.

ROSETTA said:
                        Too soon we embrace that
Impermanent appetitive flux,
Humorous and hard, which adults fear

Is real and right, the irreverent place,
The clown's cosmos.

EMBLE said:

                        Who is comforted by it?
Pent in the packed compulsory ring
Round father's frown each *famus* waits his
Day to dominate. Here a dean sits
Making bedroom eyes at a beef steak,
As wholly oral as the avid creatures
Of the celibate sea; there, sly and wise
Commuters mimic the Middle Way,
Trudging on time to a tidy fortune.
(A senator said: "From swimming-hole
To board-meeting is a big distance.")
Financiers on knolls, noses pointing
East towards oil fields, inhale the surplus
Their bowels boast of, while boys and girls, their
Hot hearts covered over with marriage
To tyrant functions, turn by degrees
To cold fish, though, precarious on the
Fringes of their feeling, a fuzzy hope
Persists somehow that sometime all this
Will walk away, and a wish gestates
For explosive pain, a punishing
Demanded moment of mortal change,
The Night of the Knock when none shall sleep,
The Absolute Instant.

QUANT said:

                        It is here, now.
For the huge wild beast of the Unexpected
Leaps on the lax recollecting back;

Unknown to him, binoculars follow
The leaping lad; lightning at noonday
Swiftly stooping to the summer-house
Engraves its disgust on engrossed flesh,
And at tea-times through tall french windows
Hurtle anonymous hostile stones.
No soul is safe. Let slight infection
Disturb a trifle some tiny gland,
And Caustic Keith grows kind and silly
Or Dainty Daisy dirties herself.
We are mocked by unmeaning; among us fall
Aimless arrows, hurting at random
As we plan to pain.

MALIN went on, spoke of the Fifth Age:
                          In peace or war,
Married or single, he muddles on,
Offending, fumbling, falling over,
And then, rather suddenly, there he is
Standing up, an astonished victor
Gliding over the good glib waters
Of the social harbor to set foot
On its welcoming shore where at last
Recognition surrounds his days with
Her felicitous light. He likes that;
He fairly blooms; his fever almost
Relaxes its hold. He learns to speak
Softer and slower, not to seem so eager;
His body acquires the blander motions
Of the approved state. His positive glow
Of fiscal health affects that unseen
Just judge, that Generalized Other
To whom he thinks and is understood by,
Who grows less gruff as if gravely impressed

By his evident air of having now
Really arrived, bereaved of every
Low relation.

EMBLE said:

        Why leave out the worst
Pang of youth? The princes of fiction,
Who ride through risks to rescue their loves,
Know their business, are not really
As young as they look. To be young means
To be all on edge, to be held waiting in
A packed lounge for a Personal Call
From Long Distance, for the low voice that
Defines one's future. The fears we know
Are of not knowing. Will nightfall bring us
Some awful order—Keep a hardware store
In a small town . . . Teach science for life to
Progressive girls—? It is getting late.
Shall we ever be asked for? Are we simply
Not wanted at all?

QUANT said:

        Well, you will soon
Not bother but acknowledge yourself
As market-made, a commodity
Whose value varies, a vendor who has
To obey his buyer, will embrace moreover
The problems put you by opposing time,
The fight with work, the feud of marriage,
Whose detonating details day and night
Invest your breathing and veto sleep,
As their own answers, like others find
The train-ride between your two natures,

The morning-evening moment when
You are free to reflect on your faults still,
Is an awkward hiatus, is indeed
The real risk to be read away with
Print and pictures, reports of what should
Never have happened, will no longer
Expect more pattern, more purpose than
Your finite fate.

ROSETTA said:
                         I refuse to accept
Your plain place, your unprivileged time.
No. No. I shall not apologize
Nor retire contempt for this tawdry age.
The juke-box jives rejoicing madly
As life after life lapses out of
Its essential self and sinks into
One press-applauded public untruth
And, massed to its music, all march in step
Led by that liar, the lukewarm Spirit
Of the Escalator, ever timely,
His whims their will, away from freedom
To a locker-room life at low tension,
Abnormal none, anonymous hosts
Driven like Danaids by drill sergeants
To ply well-paid repetitive tasks
(Dowdy they'll die who have so dimly lived)
In cosy crowds. Till the caring poet,
Child of his chamber, chooses rightly
His pleased picture of pure solitudes
Where gusts gamble over gaunt areas
Frozen and futile but far enough
From vile civilities vouched for by

Statisticians, this stupid world where
Gadgets are gods and we go on talking,
Many about much, but remain alone,
Alive but alone, belonging—where?—
Unattached as tumbleweed. Time flies.

QUANT said:

No, Time returns, a continuous Now
As the clock counts. The captain sober
Gulps his beer as the galley-boy drunk
Gives away his water; William East is
Entering Olive as Alfred West
Is leaving Elaine; Lucky McGuire
Divides the spoil as Vacuous Molly
Joins in the joke; Justice van Diemen
Foresees the day when the slaves rise and
Ragamuffins roll around the block
His cone-shaped skull, while Convict 90
Remembers his mother. We move on
As the wheel wills; one revolution
Registers all things, the rise and fall
In pay and prices, peregrinations
Of lies and loves, colossal bangs and
Their sequential quiets in quick order.
And who runs may read written on walls
Eternal truths: "Teddy Peterson
Never washes." "I'm not your father
You slobbering Swede." "Sulky Moses
Has bees in his bush." "Betty is thinner
But Connie lays."—Who closes his eyes
Sees the blonde vistas bathed in sunlight,
The temples, tombs, and terminal god,
Tall by a torrent, the etruscan landscape

Of Man's Memory. His myths of Being
Are there always. In that unchanging
Lucid lake where he looks for ever
Narcissus sees the sensitive face
He's too intelligent to trust or like,
Pleading his pardon. Polyphemus
Curses his cave or, catching a nymph,
Begs for brotherhood with a big stick,
Hobbledehoy and helpless. Kind Orpheus lies
Violently slain on the virid bank,
That smooth sward where he sinned against kind,
And, wild by the water, women stone
The broken torso but the bloody head,
In the far distance, floating away
Down the steady stream, still opening
Its charming mouth, goes chanting on in
Fortissimo tones, a tenor lyre
Dinning the doom into a deaf Nature
Of her loose chaos. For Long-ago has been
Ever-After since Ur-Papa gave
The Primal Yawn that expressed all things
(In His Boredom their beings) and brought forth
The wit of this world. One-Eye's mistake
Is sorry He spoke.

MALIN went on, spoke of the Sixth Age:
                    Our subject has changed.
He looks far from well; he has fattened on
His public perch; takes pills for vigor
And sound sleep, and sees in his mirror
The jawing genius of a jackass age,
A rich bore. When he recollects his
Designed life, the presented pomp is

A case of chaos, a constituted
Famine of effect. Feverish in
Their bony building his brain cells keep
Their hectic still, but his heart transfixed
By the ice-splinter of an ingrown tear,
Comatose in her cave, cares little
What the senses say; at the same time,
Dedicated, clandestine under
The guilt and grime of a great career,
The bruise of his boyhood is as blue still,
Horrid and hurting, hostile to his life
As a praised person. He pines for some
Nameless Eden where he never was
But where in his wishes once again
On hallowed acres, without a stitch
Of achievement on, the children play
Nor care how comely they couldn't be
Since they needn't know they're not happy.

QUANT said:

So do the ignored. In the soft-footed
Hours of darkness when elevators
Raise blondes aloft to bachelor suites
And the night-nurse notices a change
In the patient's breathing, and Pride lies
Awake in himself too weak to stir
As Shame and Regret shove into his their
Inflamed faces, we failures inquire
For the treasure also. I too have shed
The tears of parting at Traitor's Halt
Where comforts finished and kind but dull,
In low landaus and electric broughams,
Through wrought-iron gates, down rhododendron

Avenues they came, Sir Ambrose Touch,
Fat Lady Feel, Professor Howling,
Doctor Dort, dear Mrs. Pollybore,
And the Scarsdale boy with a school friend
To see us off. (But someone important,
Alas, was not there.) Some laughed of course.
Ha-ha, ha-ha, cried Hairy Mary
The lighthouse lady, little Miss Odd,
And Will Walton the watercress man,
And pointed northward. Repellent there
A storm was brewing, but we started out
In carpet-slippers by candlelight
Through Wastewood in the wane of the year,
Past Torture Tower and Twisting Ovens,
Their ruins ruled by the arrested insect
And abortive bird. In the bleak dawn
We reached Red River; on Wrynose Weir
Lay a dead salmon; when the dogs got wind
They turned tail. We talked very little;
Thunder thudded; on the thirteenth day
Our diseased guide deserted with all
The milk chocolate. Emerging from
Forest to foothills, our fears increased,
For roads grew rougher and ridges were
Congested with gibbets. We had just reached
The monastery bridge; the mist cleared;
I got one glimpse of the granite walls
And the glaciers guarding the Good Place.
(A giant jawbone jutted from that ice;
Condors on those crags coldly observed our
Helpless anguish.) My hands in my pockets,
Whistling ruefully I wandered back
By Maiden Moor and Mockbeggar Lane

To Nettlenaze where nightingales sang
Of my own evil.

ROSETTA said:

                    Yet holy are the dolls
Who, junior for ever, just begin
Their open lives in absolute space,
Are simply themselves, deceiving none,
Their clothes creatures, so clearly expressing,
Tearless, timeless, the paternal world
Of pillars and parks. O Primal Age
When we danced deisal, our dream-wishes
Vert and volant, unvetoed our song.
For crows brought cups of cold water to
Ewes that were with young; unicorn herds
Galumphed through lilies; little mice played
With great cock-a-hoop cats; courteous griffins
Waltzed with wyverns, and the wild horses
Drew nigh their neighbors and neighed with joy,
All feasting with friends. What faded you
To this drab dusk? O the drains are clogged,
Rain-rusted, the roofs of the privies
Have fallen in, the flag is covered
With stale stains and the stable-clock face
Mottled with moss. Mocking blows the wind
Into my mouth. O but they've left me.
I wronged. Then they ran. I'm running down.
Wafna. Wafna. Who's to wind me now
In this lost land?

EMBLE said:

                    I've lost the key to
The garden gate. How green it was there,
How large long ago when I looked out,

Excited by sand, the sad glitter
Of desert dreck, not dreaming I saw
My future home. It foils my magic:
Right is the ritual but wrong the time,
The place improper.

QUANT said:

                    Reproaches come,
Emanating from some hidden center,
Cold radiations directed at us
In waves unawares, and we are shaken
By a sceptical sigh from a scotch fir,
The Accuser crying in a cocktail glass.

Someone had put on the juke box a silly number *With That Thing* as played by *The Three Snorts*, and to this he sang:

Let me sell you a song, the most side-splitting tale
Since old Chaos caught young Cosmos bending
With his back bare and his braces down,
Homo Vulgaris, the Asterisk Man.

He burned all his boats and both pink ends
Of his crowing candle, cooked his goose-flesh,
Jumped his bailiwick, jilted his heirs
And pickled his piper, the Approximate Man.

With his knees to the north and the night in his stride
He advanced on the parlors, then vanished upstairs
As a bath-tub admiral to bark commands
At his ten hammer toes, the Transient Man.

Once in his while his wit erupted
One pure little puff, one pretty idea;

A fumarole since, he has fizzled a cloud
Of gossip and gas, the Guttering Man.

Soon his soul will be sent up to Secret Inks,
His body be bought by the Breakdown Gang;
It's time for the Ticklers to take him away
In a closed cab, the Camouflage Man.

So look for a laundress to lay him out cold,
A fanciful fairy to fashion his tomb
In Rest-room Roman; get ready to pray
In a wheel-chair voice for the Watery Man.

MALIN went on once more, spoke of the Seventh Age:
    His last chapter has little to say.
    He grows backward with gradual loss of
    Muscular tone and mental quickness:
    He lies down; he looks through the window
    Ailing at autumn, asks a sign but
    The afternoons are inert, none come to
    Quit his quarrel or quicken the long
    Years of yawning and he yearns only
    For total extinction. He is tired out;
    His last illusions have lost patience
    With the human enterprise. The end comes: he
    Joins the majority, the jaw-dropped
    Mildewed mob and is modest at last.
    There his case rests: let who can disprove.

So their discussion concluded. MALIN excused himself and went
to the men's room. QUANT went to the bar to fetch more drinks. RO-
SETTA and EMBLE sat silent, occupied with memories of a distant or
recent, a real or imaginary past.

ROSETTA was thinking:

> There was Lord Lugar at Lighthazels,
> Violent-tempered; he voted against
> The Banking Bill. At Brothers Intake
> Sir William Wand; his Water Treaty
> Enriched Arabia. At Rotherhope
> General Locke, a genial man who
> Kept cormorants. At Craven Ladies
> Old Tillingham-Trench; he had two passions,
> Women and walking-sticks. At Wheels Rake,
> In his low library loving Greek
> Bishop Bottrel; he came back from the East
> With a fat notebook full of antique
> Liturgies and laws, long-forgotten
> Christian creeds occluded within a
> Feldspar fortress. Fay was his daughter;
> A truant mutation, she took up art,
> Carved in crystal, became the friend of
> Green-eyed Gelert the great dressmaker,
> And died in Rome. There was Dr. Sykes
> At Mugglers Mound; his monograph on
> The chronic cough is a classic still;
> He was loved by all. At Lantern Byepew
> Susan O'Rourke, a sensitive who
> Prayed for the plants. They have perished now; their
> Level lawns and logical vistas
> Are obliterated; their big stone
> Houses are shut. Ease is rejected,
> Poor and penalized the private state.

EMBLE was thinking:

> I have friends already, faces I know
> In that calm crowd, wearing clothes like mine,

Who have settled down, accepted at once,
Contemporary with Trojan Knights
And Bronze-Age bagmen; Bud and Whitey
And Clifford Monahan and Clem Lifschutz,
Dicky Lamb, Dominic Moreno,
Svensson, Seidel: they seem already
Like anyone else. Must I end like that?

Waiting to be served, QUANT caught sight of himself again in the
bar mirror and thought:

Ingenious George reached his journey's end
Killed by a cop in a comfort station,
Dan dropped dead at his dinner table,
Mrs. O'Malley with Miss De Young
Wandered away into wild places
Where desert dogs reduced their status
To squandered bones, and it's scared you look,
Dear friend of a friend, to face me now.
How limply you've aged, how loose you stand
A frog in your fork, my far-away
Primrose prince, but a passenger here
Retreating to his tent. Whose trump hails your
Shenanigans now? Kneel to your bones
And cuddle your cough. Your castle's down.
It rains as you run, rusts where you lie.
Beware my weakness. Worse will follow.
The Blue Little Boys should blow their horns
Louder and longer, for the lost sheep
Are nibbling nightshade. But never mind . . .

MALIN returned and QUANT brought back drinks to the table.
Then raising his glass to ROSETTA, QUANT said:

Come, peregrine nymph, display your warm
Euphoric flanks in their full glory
Of liberal life; with luscious note
Smoothly sing the softer data of an
Unyielding universe, youth, money,
Liquor and love; delight your shepherds
For crazed we come and coarsened we go
Our wobbling way: there's a white silence
Of antiseptics and instruments
At both ends, but a babble between
And a shame surely. O show us the route
Into hope and health; give each the required
Pass to appease the superior archons;
Be our good guide.

To which ROSETTA answered:
                    What gift of direction
Is entrusted to me to take charge
Of an expedition any may
Suggest or join? For the journey homeward
Arriving by roads already known
At sites and sounds one has sensed before,
The knowledge needed is not special,
The sole essential a sad unrest
Which no life can lack. Long is the way
Of the Seven Stages, slow the going,
And few, maybe, are faithful to the end,
But all start out with the hope of success,
Arm in arm with their opposite type
Like dashing Adonis dressed to kill
And worn Wat with his walrus mustache,
Or one by one like Wandering Jews,
Bullet-headed bandit, broad churchman,

Lobbyist, legatee, loud virago,
Uncle and aunt and alien cousin,
Mute or maddening through the Maze of Time,
Seek its center, desiring like us
The Quiet Kingdom. Comfort your wills then
With hungry hopes; to this indagation
Allay your longings: may our luck find the
Regressive road to Grandmother's House.

As everyone knows, many people reveal in a state of semi-intoxication capacities which are quite beyond them when they are sober: the shy talk easily and brilliantly to total strangers, the stammerers get through complicated sentences without a hitch, the unathletic is translated into a weight-lifter or a sprinter, the prosaic show an intuitive grasp of myth and symbol. A less noted and a more significant phenomenon, however, is the way in which our faith in the existence of other selves, normally rather wobbly, is greatly strengthened and receives, perhaps precisely because, for once, doubt is so completely overcome, the most startling justifications. For it can happen, if circumstances are otherwise propitious, that members of a group in this condition establish a rapport in which communication of thoughts and feelings is so accurate and instantaneous, that they appear to function as a single organism.

So it was now as they sought that state of prehistoric happiness which, by human beings, can only be imagined in terms of a landscape bearing a symbolic resemblance to the human body. The more completely these four forgot their surroundings and lost their sense of time, the more sensitively aware of each other they became, until they achieved in their dream that rare community which is otherwise only attained in states of extreme wakefulness. But this did not happen all at once.

PART THREE

The Seven Stages

O Patria, patria! Quanto mi costi!

A. GHISLANZONI *Aida*

At first all is dark and each walks alone. What they share is only the feelings of remoteness and desertion, of having marched for miles and miles, of having lost their bearings, of a restless urge to find water. Gradually for each in turn the darkness begins to dissolve and their vision to take shape.

QUANT is the first to see anything. He says:

> Groping through fog, I begin to hear
> A salt lake lapping:
> Dotterels and dunlins on its dark shores
> Scurry this way and that.

Now ROSETTA perceives clearly and says:

> In the center of a sad plain
> Without forests or footpaths,
> Rimmed with rushes and moss
> I see a tacit tarn.
>
> Some oddling angler in summer
> May visit the spot, or a spy
> Come here to cache a stolen
> Map or meet a rival.
>
> But who remarks the beehive mounds,
> Graves of creatures who cooked
> And wanted to be worshipped and perhaps
> Were the first to feel our sorrow?

And now MALIN:

> How still it is; our horses
> Have moved into the shade, our mothers
> Have followed their migrating gardens.
>
> Curlews on kettle moraines
> Foretell the end of time,
> The doom of paradox.
>
> But lovelorn sighs ascend
> From wretched greedy regions
> Which cannot include themselves;
>
> And a freckled orphan flinging
> Ducks and drakes at a pond,
> Stops looking for stones,
>
> And wishes he were a steamboat
> Or Lugalzaggisi, the loud
> Tyrant of Erech and Umma.

And last EMBLE:

> The earth looks woeful and wet;
> On the raw horizon regiments pass
> Tense against twilight, tired beneath
> Their corresponsive spears.
>
> Slogging on through slush
> By broken bridges and burnt hamlets
> Where the starving stand, staring past them
> At remote indelible hills.

And now, though separate still, they begin to advance from their several starting-points into the same mountainous district. ROSETTA says:

Now peaks oppose to the ploughman's march
   Their twin confederate forms,
In a warm weather, white with lilies,
   Evergreen for grazing.
Smooth the surfaces, sweeping the curves
   Of these comely frolic clouds,
Where the great go to forget themselves,
   The beautiful and boon to die.

QUANT says:

     Lights are moving
     On domed hills
     Where little monks
     Get up in the dark.

     Though wild volcanoes
     Growl in their sleep
     At a green world,
     Inside their cloisters

     They sit translating
     A vision into
     The vulgar lingo
     Of armed cities,

     Where bridges arrive
     Through great doors,
     And robbers' bones
     Dangle from gallows.

EMBLE says:

     Bending forward
     With stern faces,
     Pilgrims puff

Up the steep bank
In huge hats.

Shouting, I run
In the other direction,
Cheerful, unchaste,
With open shirt
And tinkling guitar.

MALIN says:

Looming over my head
Mountains menace my life,
But on either hand, let down
From U-valleys like yarn,
Waterfalls all the way
Quietly encourage me on.

And now one by one they enter the same valley and begin to ascend the same steep pass. ROSETTA is in front, then EMBLE, then MALIN and QUANT last.

ROSETTA says:

These hills may be hollow; I've a horror of dwarfs
And a streaming cold.

EMBLE says:

This stony pass
Is bad for my back. My boots are too small
My haversack too heavy. I hate my knees
But like my legs.

MALIN says:

The less I feel
The more I mind. I should meet death
With great regret.

QUANT says:

                    Thank God I was warned
        To bring an umbrella and had bribes enough
        For the red-haired rascals, for the reservoir guard
        A celluloid sandwich, and silk eggs
        For the lead smelters; for Lizzie O'Flynn,
        The capering cowgirl with clay on her hands,
        Tasty truffles in utopian jars,
        And dungarees with Danish buttons
        For Shilly and Shally the shepherd kings.

Now ROSETTA says:

        The ground's aggression is growing less.
        The clouds are clearing.

EMBLE says:

                        My cape is dry.
        I can reckon correctly.

MALIN says:

                        My real intentions
        Are nicer now.

And QUANT says:

                    I'm nearing the top.
        When I hear what I'm up to, how I shall laugh.

    And so, on a treeless watershed, at the tumbledown Mariners Tav-
ern (which is miles inland) the four assemble, having completed the
first stage of their journey. They look about them, and everything
seems somehow familiar. EMBLE says:

        The railroads like the rivers run for the most part
            East and west, and from here

On a clear day both coasts are visible
    And the long piers of their ports.
To the south one sees the sawtooth range
    Our nickel and copper come from,
And beyond it the Barrens used for Army
    Manœuvres; while to the north
A brown blur of buildings marks
    Some sacred or secular town.

MALIN says:

Every evening the oddest collection
    Of characters crowd this inn:
Here a face from a farm, its frankness yearning
    For corruption and riches; there
A gaunt gospel whom grinning miners
    Will stone to death by a dolmen;
Heroes confess to whores, detectives
    Chat or play chess with thieves.

QUANT says:

And one finds it hard to fall asleep here.
    Lying awake and listening
To the creak of new creeds on the kitchen stairs
    Or the sob of a dream next door,
(By pass and port they percolated,
    By friendships and official channels)
Gentler grows the heart, gentler and much
    Less certain it will succeed.

But ROSETTA says impatiently:

Questioned by these crossroads our common hope
Replies we must part; in pairs proceed

By bicycle, barge, or bumbling local,
As vagabonds or in wagon-lits,
On weedy waters, up winding lanes,
Down rational roads the Romans built,
Over or into, under or round
Mosses dismal or mountains sudden,
Farmlands or fenlands or factory towns,
Left and right till the loop be complete
And we meet once more.

EMBLE whispers to himself:

                    Do I mind with whom?
Yes, a great deal.

And MALIN:

                  In youth I would have cared,
But not now

And QUANT:

                I know what will happen,
Am sincerely sorry.

They divide thus, youth with youth and age with age. To the left go ROSETTA and EMBLE, to the right QUANT and MALIN, these on foot, those by car, moving outwards in opposite directions from the high heartland to the maritime plains.

EMBLE says:

          As I pull on my gloves and prepare
          For another day-long drive,
          The landscape is full of life:
          Nieces of millionaires
          Twitter on terraces,

Peasant wives are pounding
Linen on stones by a stream,
And a doctor's silk hat dances
On top of a hedge as he hurries
Along a sunken lane.

All these and theirs are at home,
May love or hate their age
And the beds they are built to fit;
Only I have no work
But my endless journey, its joy
The whirr of wheels, the hiss
As moonlit miles flash by,
Its grief the glimpse of a face
Whose unique beauty cannot
Be asked to alter with me.

Or must everyone see himself
As I, as the pilgrim prince
Whose life belongs to his quest
For the Truth, the tall princess,
The buried gold or the Grail,
The important thought-of Thing
Which is never here and now
Like this world through which he goes
That all the others appear
To possess the secret of?

QUANT says:

Between pollarded poplars
This rural road
Ambles downhill
In search of the sea.

Nothing, neither
The farms nor the flowers,
The cows nor the clouds,
Look restive or wrong.

Then why without warning,
In my old age,
My duty done,
Do I change to a child,

And shake with shame,
Afraid of Father,
Demanding Mother's
Forgiveness again?

ROSETTA says:

The light collaborates with a land of ease,
    And rivers meander at random
Through meadowsweet massed on moist pastures,
    Past decrepit palaces
Where, brim from belvederes, bred for riding
    And graceful dancing, gaze
Fine old families who fear dishonor.

But modern on the margin of marshy ground
    Glitter the glassier homes
Of more practical people with plainer minds,
    And along the vacationer's coast,
Distributed between its hotels and casinos,
    Ex-monarchs remember a past
Of wars and waltzes as they wait for death.

MALIN says:

        Though dunes still hide from the eye
            The shining shore,

Already by a certain exciting
Kind of discomfort
I know the ocean near.

For wind and whining gull
Are saying something,
Or trying to say, about time
And the anxious heart
Which a matter-snob would dismiss.

So, arriving two and two at rival ports, they complete the second
stage of their journey.

ROSETTA says:

These ancient harbors are hailed by the morning
Light that untidies
Warehouses and wharves and wilder rocks
Where intolerant lives
Fight and feed in the fucoid thickets
Of popular pools.

EMBLE says:

Reflected fleets, feeling in awe
Of their sheltered lagoon
Stand still, a steady congregation
Of gigantic shadows;
Derricks on these docks adore in silence
The noon they denote.

MALIN says:

Quiet falls the dusk at this queasy juncture
Of water and earth,
And lamps are lit on the long esplanade;
Urgent whispers

Promise peace, and impatience shakes
   Ephemeral flesh.

And QUANT says:
   As, far from furniture and formal gardens
     The desperate spirit
  Thinks of its end in the third person,
     As a speck drowning
  In those wanton mansions where the whales take
     Their huge fruitions.

But here they may not linger long. EMBLE says to ROSETTA:

A private plane, its propeller tied
With red ribbons is ready waiting
To take us to town.

MALIN says to QUANT:
        A train whistles
For the last time. We must leave at once.

And so by air, by rail, they turn inland again towards a common
goal.

QUANT says:
  Autumn has come early; evening falls;
  Our train is traversing at top speed
  A pallid province of puddles and stumps
  Where helpless objects, an orphaned quarry,
  A waif of a works, a widowed engine,
  For a sorry second sigh and are gone
  As we race through the rain with rattling windows
  Bound for a borough all bankers revere.

ROSETTA says:

> Lulled by an engine's hum,
> Our insulated lives
> Go floating freely through
> Space in a metal spore.
>
> White hangs the waning moon,
> A scruple in the sky,
> And constellations crowd
> Our neighborhood the night.

QUANT says:

> In the smoking cars all seats are taken
> By melancholics mewed in their dumps,
> Elegant old-school ex-lieutenants
> Cashiered for shuddering, short blowhards,
> Thwarted geniuses in threadbare coats,
> Once well-to-do's at their wit's end,
> And underpaid agents of underground powers,
> The faded and failing in flight towards town.

ROSETTA says:

> Just visible but vague,
> Way down below us lies
> The world of hares and hounds,
> Open to our contempt.
>
> Escaping by our skill
> Its public prison, we
> Could love ourselves and live
> In just anarchic joy.

QUANT says:

> The parlor cars and Pullmans are packed also
> With scented assassins, salad-eaters

Who murder on milk, merry expressives,
Pert pyknics with pumpkin heads,
Clever cardinals with clammy hands,
Jolly logicians with juvenile books,
Farmers, philistines, *filles-de-joie*,
The successful smilers the city can use.

ROSETTA says:

What fear of freedom then
Causes our clasping hands
To make in miniature
That earth anew, and now

By choice instead of chance
To suffer from the same
Attraction and untruth,
Suspicion and respect?

QUANT says:

What mad oracle could have made us believe
The capital will be kind when the country is not,
And value our vanities, provide our souls
With play and pasture and permanent water?

They lose altitude, they slow down, they arrive at the city, having completed the third stage of the journey, and are united once more, greet each other.

EMBLE says:

Here we are.

MALIN says:

As we hoped we have come
Together again.

ROSETTA says:

> I am glad, I think.
> It is fun to be four.

QUANT says:

> The flushed animations
> Of crowds and couples look comic to friends.

They look about them with great curiosity. Then MALIN says:

> The scene has all the signs of a facetious culture,
> Publishing houses, pawnshops and pay-toilets;
> August and Graeco-Roman are the granite temples
> Of the medicine men whose magic keeps this body
>   Politic free from fevers,
>   Cancer and constipation.

> . The rooms near the railroad-station are rented mainly
> By the criminally inclined; the Castle is open on Sundays;
> There are parks for plump and playgrounds for pasty children;
> The police must be large, but little men are hired to
>   Service the subterranean
>   Miles of dendritic drainage.

> A married tribe commutes, mild from suburbia,
> Whom ritual rules protect against raids by the nomad
> Misfortunes they fear; for they flinch in
>   their dreams at the scratch
> Of coarse pecuniary claws, at crying images,
>   Petulant, thin, reproachful,
>   Destitute shades of dear ones

> Well, here I am but how, how, asks the visitor,
> Strolling through the strange streets, can I start to discover
> The fashionable feminine fret, or the form of insult
> Minded most by the men? In what myth do their sages

Locate the cause of evil?
How are these people punished?

How, above all, will they end? By any natural
Fascination of frost or flood, or from the artful
Obliterating bang whereby God's rebellious image
After thousands of thankless years spent in thinking about it,
    Finally finds a solid
    Proof of its independence?

Now a trolley car comes, going northward. They take it. EMBLE says:

This torturous route through town
Was planned, it seems, to serve
Its institutions; for we halt
With a jerk at the Gothic gates
Of the Women's Prison, the whitewashed
Hexagonal Orphanage for
Doomed Children, the driveway,
Bordered with trees in tubs
Of the Orthopædic Hospital,
And are crowded by the close relatives
Of suffering, who sit upright
With little offerings on their laps
Of candy, magazines, comics,
Avoiding each other's eyes,
Shy of a rival shame.

Slums are replaced by suburbs,
Suburbs by tennis-courts, tennis-courts
By greenhouses and vegetable gardens.
The penultimate stop is the State
Asylum, a large Palladian
Edifice in acres of grounds

Surrounded by iron railings;
And now there is no one left
For the final run through fields
But ourselves whose diseases as yet
Are undiagnosed, and the driver
Who is anxious to get home to his tea.

The buttercups glitter; our bell
Clangs loudly; and the lark's
Song is swallowed up in
The blazing blue: we are set
Down and do not care
Very much but wonder why.

Now they see before them, standing, half hidden by trees, on a little insurrection of red sandstone above a coiling river, the big house which marks the end of their journey's fourth stage. ROSETTA is enthusiastic and runs forward saying:

In I shall go, out I shall look.

But the others are tired and MALIN says:

Very well, we will wait, watch from outside.

QUANT says:
A scholarly old scoundrel
Whose fortune was founded on the follies of others,
    Built it for his young bride.
She died in childbed; he died on the gallows;
    The property passed to the Crown.

    The façade has a lifeless look,
For no one uses the enormous ballroom;

But in book-lined rooms at the back
Committees meet, and many strange
　　Decisions are secretly taken.

　　High up in the East Tower,
A pale-faced widow looks pensively down
　　At the terrace outside where the snow
Flutters and flurries round the formal heads
　　Of statues that stare at the park.

　　And the guards at the front gate
Change with the seasons; in cheerful Spring
　　How engaging their glances; but how
Morose in Fall: ruined kitchen-maids
　　Blubber behind the bushes.

ROSETTA returns, more slowly than she left. EMBLE asks:
　　Well, how was it? What did you see?

ROSETTA answers:
　　Opera glasses on the ormolu table
　　Frock-coated father framed on the wall
　　In a bath-chair facing a big bow-window,
　　With valley and village invitingly spread,
　　　　I got what is going on.

　　At the bend of the Bourne where the brambles grow thickest
　　Major Mott joins Millicent Rusk;
　　Discreetly the kingfisher keeps his distance
　　But an old cob swan looks on as they
　　　　Commit the sanguine sin.

　　Heavy the orchards; there's Alison pinching
　　Her baby brother, Bobby and Dick
　　Frying a frog with their father's reading-glass,

Conrad and Kay in the carpentry shed
  Where they've no business to be.

Cold are the clays of Kibroth-Hattavah,
Babel's urbanities buried in sand,
Red the geraniums in the rectory garden
Where the present incumbent reads Plato in French
  And has lost his belief in Hell.

From the gravel-pits in Groaning Hollow
To the monkey-puzzle on Murderer's Hill.
From the Wellington Arms to the white steam laundry,
The significant note is nature's cry
  Of long-divided love.

I have watched through a window a World that is fallen,
The mating and malice of men and beasts,
The corporate greed of quiet vegetation,
And the homesick little obstinate sobs
  Of things thrown into being.

  I would gladly forget; let us go quickly.

EMBLE said:
  Yonder, look, is a yew avenue,
  A mossy mile. For amusement's sake
  Let us run a race till we reach the end.

  This, willing or unwilling, they start to do and, as they run, their
rival natures, by art comparing and compared, reveal themselves.
Thus MALIN mutters:

  "Alas," say my legs, "if we lose it will be
  A sign you have sinned."

And QUANT:

                   The safest place
    Is the more or less middling: the mean average
    Is not noticed.

And EMBLE:

                 How nice it feels
    To be out ahead: I'm always lucky
    But must remember how modest to look.

And ROSETTA:

    Let them call; I don't care. I shall keep them waiting.
    They ought to have helped me. I can't hope to be first
    So let me be last.

In this manner, sooner or later they come to the crumbling lichen-covered wall of the forgotten graveyard which marks the end of the fifth stage of their journey. At their feet lies a fallen wooden sign, bearing in faded letters the warning:

No Entrance Here Without a Subject

and underneath this, in smaller, barely decipherable script, some verses which EMBLE starts to read aloud:

    Stranger, this still
    Museum exhibits
    The results of life:
    Thoughtfully, therefore,
    Peer as you pass
    These cases clouded
    By vetch and eyebright

And viper's bugloss
At each little collection
Loosely arranged
Of dated dust.

Here it is holy,
Here at last
In mute marble
The Master closed
His splendid period;
A spot haunted
By goat-faced grasshoppers
And gangling boys
Taunted by talents
Which tell them more
Than their flesh can feel.
Here impulse loses
Its impetus: thus
Far and no farther
Their legs, resolutions
And longings carried
The big, the ambitious,
The beautiful; all
Stopped in mid-stride
At this straggling border
Where wildflowers begin
And wealth ends.

Yet around their rest
Flittermice, finches
And flies restore
Their lost milieu;
An inconsequential
Host of pert

Occasional creatures,
Blindly, playfully,
Bridging death's
Eternal gap
With quotidian joy.

MALIN sighs and says what they are all thinking but wish they were not.

Again we must digress, go by different
Paths in pairs to explore the land.

Knowing they will never be able to agree as to who shall accompany whom, they cast lots and so it falls out that ROSETTA is to go with QUANT and EMBLE with MALIN. Two are disappointed, two are disturbed.

QUANT mutters:
This bodes badly.

And MALIN:
So be it. Who knows
If we wish what we will?

And ROSETTA:
Will you forget
If you know that I won't?

And EMBLE:
Will your need be me?

They depart now, MALIN and EMBLE westward on bicycles, QUANT and ROSETTA eastward by boat, sad through fair scenes, thinking of another and talking to themselves.

MALIN says:

> As we cycle silent through a serious land
> For hens and horses, my hunger for a live
> Person to father impassions my sense
> Of this boy's beauty in battle with time.
>
> These old-world hamlets and haphazard lanes
> Are perilous places; how plausible here
> All arcadian cult of carnal perfection,
> How intoxicating the platonic myth.

EMBLE says:

> Pleasant my companion but I pine for another.

QUANT says:

> Our canoe makes no noise; monotonous
> Ramparts of reeds surround our navigation;
> The waterway winds as it wants through the hush:
> O fortunate fluid her fingers caress.
>
> Welcome her, world; sedge-warblers, betray your
> Hiding places with song; and eddy, butterflies,
> In frivolous flights about that fair head:
> How apt your homage to her innocent disdain.

ROSETTA says:

> The figure I prefer is far away.

MALIN says:

> To know nature is not enough for the ego;
> The aim of its eros is to create a soul,
> The start of its magic is stolen flesh.

QUANT says:

> Let nature unite us whose needs belong to
> Separate systems that make no sense to each other:
> She is not my sister and I am not her friend.

EMBLE says:

> Unequal our happiness: his is greater.

ROSETTA says:

> Lovelier would this look if my love were with me.

MALIN says:

> Girlishly glad that my glance is not chaste,
> He wants me to want what he would refuse:
> For sons have this desire for a slave also.

QUANT says:

> Both graves of the stream are agog as here
> Comes a bride for a bridegroom in a boat ferried
> By a dying man dreaming of a daughter-wife.

Now they arrive, two and two, east and west, at the hermetic gardens and the sixth stage of their journey is completed. They gaze about them entranced at the massive mildness of these survivals from an age of cypresses and cisterns.

ROSETTA says:

> How tempting to trespass in these Italian gardens
> With their smirk ouches and sweet-smelling borders,
>   To lean on the low
> Parapet of some pursive fountain
>   And drowse through the unctuous day.

EMBLE says:

> There are special perspectives for speculation,
> Random rose-walks, and rustic bridges
>> Over neat canals;
> A miniature railroad with mossy halts
>> Wambles through wanton groves.

QUANT says:

> Yet this is a theater where thought becomes act
> And beside a sundial, in the silent umbrage
>> Of some dark daedal,
> The ruined rebel is recreated
>> And chooses a chosen self.

> From lawns and relievos the leisure makes
> Its uncomfortable claim and, caught off its guard,
>> His hardened heart
> Consents to suffer, and the sudden instant
>> Touches his time at last.

MALIN says:

> Tense on the parterre, he takes the hero's
> Leap into love; then, unlatching the wicket
>> Gate he goes:
> The plains of his triumph appear empty,
>> But now among their motionless

> Avenues and urns with extra élan
> Faster revolves the invisible corps
>> Of pirouetting angels,
> And a chronic chorus of cascades and birds
>> Cuts loose in a wild cabaletta.

Presently the extraordinary charm of these gardens begins to work upon them also. It seems an accusation. They become uneasy and unwell.

EMBLE says:

> I would stay to be saved but the stillness here
> Reminds me too much of my mother's grief:
> It scorns and scares me.

QUANT says:

> My excuses throb
> Louder and lamer.

ROSETTA says:

> The long shadows
> Disapprove of my person.

MALIN says:

> Reproached by the doves,
> My groin groans.

ROSETTA:

> I've got a headache,
> And my nose is inflamed.

QUANT:

> My knees are stiff.

EMBLE:

> My teeth need attention.

Then QUANT says:

> Who will trust me now,
> Who with broad jokes have bored my children
> And, warm by my wife, have wished her dead
> Yet turned her over, who have told strangers
> Of the cars and castles that accrued with the fortune
> I might have made?

And EMBLE says:

>   My mortal body
>   Has sinned on sofas; assigning to each
>   Points for pleasure, I have pencilled on envelopes
>   Lists of my loves.

And ROSETTA says:

>   Alas for my sneers
>   At the poor and plain: I must pay for thinking
>   Failure funny.

And MALIN says:

>   I have felt too good
>   At being better than the best of my colleagues:
>   Walking by water, have worked out smiling
>   Deadly reviews. My deeds forbid me
>   To linger longer. I'll leave my friend,
>   Be sorry by myself.

Then EMBLE again:

>   I must slip off
>   To the woods to worry.

Then ROSETTA:

>   I want to retire
>   To some private place and pray to be made
>   A good girl.

And then QUANT:

>   I must go away
>   With my terrors until I have taught them to sing.

So one by one they plunge into the labyrinthine forest and vanish down solitary paths, with no guide but their sorrows, no companion but their own voices. Their ways cross and recross yet never once do they meet though now and then one catches somewhere not far off a brief snatch of another's song. Thus QUANT's voice is heard singing:

> A vagrant veteran I,
> Discharged with grizzled chin,
> · Sans youth or use, sans uniform,
> A tiger turned an ass.

Then MALIN's:

> These branches deaf and dumb
> Were woeful suitors once;
> Mourning unmanned, and moping turned
> Their sullen souls to wood.

Then ROSETTA's:

> My dress is torn, my tears
> Are running as I run
> Through forests far from father's eyes
> To look for a true love.

Then EMBLE's:

> My mother weeps for me
> Who disappeared at play
> From home and hope like all who chase
> The blue elusive bird.

Now QUANT's again:

> Through gloomy woods I go
> Ex-demigod; the damp
> Awakes my wound; I want my tea
> But needed am of none.

Now EMBLE's:

>   More faint, more far away
>   The huntsman's social horn
>   Call through the cold uncanny woods
>   And nearer draws the night.

Now ROSETTA's:

>   Dear God, regard thy child
>   Repugn or pacify
>   All furry forms and fangs that lurk
>   Within this horrid shade.

Now MALIN's:

>   Their given names forgot,
>   Mere species of despair,
>   On whims of wind their wills depend,
>   On temperatures their mood.

And yet once more QUANT's:

>   So, whistling as I walk
>   Through brake and copse, I keep
>   A lookout for the Limping One
>   Who buys abandoned souls.

Obedient to their own mysterious laws of direction, their twisting paths converge, approach their several voices, and collect the four for a startled reunion at the forest's edge. They stare at what they see.

QUANT says:

>   The climate of enclosure, the cool forest
>   Break off abruptly:
>   Giddy with the glare and ungoverned heat,

We stop astonished,
Interdicted by desert, its dryness edged
    By a scanty shrub
Of Joshua trees and giant cacti;
    Then, vacant of value,
Incoherent and infamous sands,
    Rainless regions
Swarming with serpents, ancestral wastes,
    Lands beyond love.

Now, with only the last half of the seventh stage to go to finish their journey, for the first time fear and doubt dismay them. Is triumph possible? If so, are they chosen? Is triumph worth it? If so, are they worthy?

MALIN says:

Boring and bare of shade,
Devoid of souvenirs and voices,
It takes will to cross this waste

Which is really empty: the mirage
Need not be tasty to tempt;
For the senses arouse themselves,

And an image of humpbacked girls
Or plates of roasted rats
Can make the mouth water.

With nothing to know about,
The mind reflects on its movements
And so doubles any distance.

Even if we had time
To read through all the wrinkled
Reports of explorers who claim

That hidden arrant streams
Chuckle through this chapped land
In profound and meager fissures,

Or that this desert is dotted with
Oases where acrobats dwell
Who make unbelievable leaps,

We should never have proof they were not
Deceiving us. For the only certain
Truth is that they returned,

And that we cannot be deaf to the question:
"Do I love this world so well
That I have to know how it ends?"

EMBLE says:

As yet the young hero's
Brow is unkissed by battle,
But he knows how necessary
Is his defiance of fate
And, serene already, he sails
Down the gorge between the august
Faces carved in the cliffs
Towards the lordship of the world.

And the gentle majority are not
Afraid either, but, owl-like
And sedate in their glass globes
The wedded couples wave
At the bandits racing by
With affection, and the learned relax
On pinguid plains among
A swarm of flying flowers.

But otherwise is it with the play
Of the child whom chance decrees
To say what all men suffer:
For he wishes against his will
To be lost, and his fear leads him
To dales of driving rain
Where peasants with penthouse eyebrows
Sullenly guard the sluices

And his steps follow the stream
Past rusting apparatus
To its gloomy beginning, the original
Chasm where brambles block
The entrance to the underworld;
There the silence blesses his sorrow,
And holy to his dread is that dark
Which will neither promise nor explain.

ROSETTA says:

Are our dreams indicative? Does it exist,
    That last landscape
Of gloom and glaciers and great storms
Where, cold into chasms, cataracts
    Topple, and torrents
Through rocky ruptures rage for ever
In a winter twilight watched by ravens,
    Birds on basalt,
And shadows of ships long-shattered lie,
Preserved disasters, in the solid ice
    Of frowning fjords?
Does the Moon's message mean what it says:
"In that oldest and most hidden of all places
    Number is unknown"?

> Can lying lovers believe their bones'
>   Unshaken assurance
> That all the elegance, all the promise
> Of the world they wish is waiting there?

Even while she is still speaking, their fears are confirmed, their hopes denied. For the world from which their journey has been one long flight rises up before them now as if the whole time it had been hiding in ambush, only waiting for the worst moment to reappear to its fugitives in all the majesty of its perpetual fury.

QUANT says:

> My shoulders shiver. A shadow chills me
> As thunderheads threaten the sun.

MALIN says:

> Righteous wrath is raising its hands
> To strike and destroy.

EMBLE says:

>   Storm invades
> The Euclidean calm. The clouds explode.
> The scene dissolves, is succeeded by
> A grinning gap, a growth of nothing
> Pervaded by vagueness.

ROSETTA says:

>   Violent winds
> Tear us apart. Terror scatters us
> To the four coigns. Faintly our sounds
> Echo each other, unrelated
> Groans of grief at a great distance.

QUANT says:

> In the wild West they are whipping each other.

EMBLE says:

> In the hungry East they are eating their books.

ROSETTA says:

> In the numb North there are no more cradles.

MALIN says:

> The sullen South has been set on fire.

EMBLE says:

> Dull through the darkness, indifferent tongues
> From bombed buildings, from blacked-out towns,
> Camps and cockpits, from cold trenches,
> Submarines and cells, recite in unison
> A common creed, declaring their weak
> Faith in confusion. The floods are rising;
> Rain ruins on the routed fragments
> Of all the armies; indistinct
> Are friend and foe, one flux of bodies
> Miles from mother, marriage, or any
> Workable world.

QUANT says:

> The wall is fallen
> That Balbus built, and back they come
> The Dark Ones to dwell in the statues,
> Manias in marble, messengers from
> The Nothing who nothings. Night descends;
> Through thickening darkness thin uneases,
> Ravenous unreals, perambulate
> Our paths and pickles.

MALIN says:

> The primary colors
> Are all mixed up; the whole numbers
> Have broken down, the big situations
> Ceased to excite.

ROSETTA says:

> Sick of time,
> Long Ada and her Eleven Daughters,
> The standing stones, stagger, disrupt
> Their petrified polka on Pillicock Mound;
> The chefs and shepherds have shot themselves,
> The dowagers dropped in their Dutch gardens,
> The battle-axe and the bosomed war-horse
> Swept grand to their graves. Graven on all things,
> Inscribed on skies, escarpments, trees,
> Notepaper, neckties, napkin rings,
> Brickwalls and barns, or branded into
> The livid limbs of lambs and men,
> Is the same symbol, the signature
> Of reluctant allegiance to a lost cause.

MALIN says:

> Our ideas have got drunk and drop their H's.

EMBLE:

> We err what we are as if we were not.

ROSETTA:

> The honest and holy are hissed at the races.

QUANT:

> God's in his greenhouse, his geese in the world.

Saying this, they woke up and recognized where they sat and who they were. The darkness which had invaded their dream was explained, for it was closing time and the bartender was turning off the lights. What they had just dreamed they could no longer recall exactly, but when EMBLE and ROSETTA looked at each other, they were conscious of some sweet shared secret which it might be dangerous to remember too well. Perhaps it was this which prompted ROSETTA to suggest that they all come back to her apartment for a snack and a nightcap for, when they accepted, she realized that she had been expecting QUANT and MALIN to decline. But it was too late now. They were out in the street already and EMBLE had hailed a cab.

PART FOUR

The Dirge

His mighty work for the nation,
Strengthening peace and securing union,
Always at it since on the throne,
Has saved the country more than one billion.
BROADSHEET *on the death of King Edward VII*

As they drove through the half-lit almost empty streets, the effect of their dream had not yet worn off but persisted as a mutual mood of discouragement. Whether they thought of Nature, of her unending stream of irrelevant events without composition or center, her reckless waste of value, her alternate looks of idiotic inertia and insane ferocity, or whether they thought of Man, of the torpor of his spirit, the indigent dryness of his soul, his bottomless credulity, his perverse preference for the meretricious or the insipid—it seemed impossible to them that either could have survived so long had not some semi-divine stranger with superhuman powers, some Gilgamesh or Napoleon, some Solon or Sherlock Holmes, appeared from time to time to rescue both, for a brief bright instant, from their egregious destructive blunders. And for such a great one who, long or lately, has always died or disappeared, they now lamented thus.

Sob, heavy world,
Sob as you spin
Mantled in mist, remote from the happy:
The washerwomen have wailed all night,
The disconsolate clocks are crying together,

And the bells toll and toll
For tall Agrippa who touched the sky:
    Shut is that shining eye
Which enlightened the lampless and lifted up
The flat and foundering, reformed the weeds
Into civil cereals and sobered the bulls;
    Away the cylinder seal,
The didactic digit and dreaded voice
Which imposed peace on the pullulating
Primordial mess. Mourn for him now,
    Our lost dad,
    Our colossal father.

    For seven cycles
    For seven years
Past vice and virtue, surviving both,
Through pluvial periods, paroxysms
Of wind and wet, through whirlpools of heat,
    And comas of deadly cold,
On an old white horse, an ugly nag,
    In his faithful youth he followed
The black ball as it bowled downhill
On the spotted spirit's spiral journey,
Its purgative path to that point of rest
    Where longing leaves it, and saw
Shimmering in the shade the shrine of gold,
The magical marvel no man dare touch,
Between the towers the tree of life
    And the well of wishes
    The waters of joy.

    Then he harrowed hell,
    Healed the abyss

Of torpid instinct and trifling flux,
Laundered it, lighted it, made it lovable with
Cathedrals and theories; thanks to him
    Brisker smells abet us,
Cleaner clouds accost our vision
    And honest sounds our ears.
For he ignored the Nightmares and annexed their ranges,
Put the clawing Chimaeras in cold storage,
Berated the Riddle till it roared and fled,
    Won the Battle of Whispers,
Stopped the Stupids, stormed into
The Fumblers' Forts, confined the Sulky
To their drab ditches and drove the Crashing
    Bores to their bogs,
    Their beastly moor.

    In the high heavens,
    The ageless places,
Their gods are wringing their great worn hands
For their watchman is away, their world-engine
Creaking and cracking. Conjured no more
    By his master music to wed
Their truths to times, the Eternal Objects
    Drift about in a daze:
O the lepers are loose in Lombard Street,
The rents are rising in the river basins,
The insects are angry. Who will dust
    The cobwebbed kingdoms now?
For our lawgiver lies below his people,
Bigger bones of a better kind,
Unwrapped by their weight, as white limestone
    Under green grass,
    The grass that fades.

But now the cab stopped at ROSETTA's apartment house. As they
went up in the elevator, they were silent but each was making a secret
resolve to banish such gloomy reflection and become, or at least ap-
pear, carefree and cheerful.

PART FIVE

The Masque

"Oh, Heaven help me," she prayed,
to be decorative and to do right."
RONALD FIRBANK *The Flower beneath the Foot*

ROSETTA had shown the men where everything was and, as they trot-
ted between the kitchen and the living room, cutting sandwiches and
fixing drinks, all felt that it was time something exciting happened
and decided to do their best to see that it did. Had they been perfectly
honest with themselves, they would have had to admit that they were
tired and wanted to go home alone to bed. That they were not was in
part due, of course, to vanity, the fear of getting too old to want fun or
too ugly to get it, but also to unselfishness, the fear of spoiling the fun
for others. Besides, only animals who are below civilization and the
angels who are beyond it can be sincere. Human beings are, necessar-
ily, actors who cannot become something before they have first pre-
tended to be it; and they can be divided, not into the hypocritical and
the sincere, but into the sane who know they are acting and the mad
who do not. So it was now as ROSETTA switched on the radio which
said:

> *Music past midnight. For men in the armed*
> *Forces on furlough and their feminine consorts,*
> *For war-workers and women in labor,*
> *For Bohemian artists and owls of the night,*
> *We present a series of savage selections*
> *By brutal bands from bestial tribes,*
> *The Quaraquorams and the Quaromanlics,*

The Arsocids and the Alonites,
The Ghuzz, the Guptas, the gloomy Krimchaks,
The Timurids and Torguts, with terrible cries
Will drag you off to their dream retreats
To dance with your deaths till the dykes collapse.

EMBLE asked ROSETTA to dance. The others sat watching. QUANT waved his cigar in time to the music and sang a verse from an old prospector's ballad.

When Laura lay on her ledger side
And nicely threw her north cheek up,
How pleasing the plight of her promising grove
And how rich the random I reached with a rise.

Whereupon MALIN sang a verse of a folksong from a Fen District.

When in wan hope I wandered away and alone,
How brag were the birds, how buxom the sky,
But sad were the sallows and slow were the brooks
And how dismal that day when I danced with my dear.

Moving well together to the music, ROSETTA and EMBLE were becoming obviously attracted to each other. In times of war even the crudest kind of positive affection between persons seems extraordinarily beautiful, a noble symbol of the peace and forgiveness of which the whole world stands so desperately in need. So to dancers and spectators alike, this quite casual attraction seemed and was of immense importance.

ROSETTA and EMBLE sang together:

Hushed is the lake of hawks
Bright with our excitement,
And all the sky of skulls
Glows with scarlet roses;

The melter of men and salt
Admires the drinker of iron:
Bold banners of meaning
Blaze o'er the host of days.

MALIN had been building a little altar of sandwiches. Now he placed an olive upon it and invoked the Queen of love.

Hasten earthward, Heavenly Venus,
Mistress of motion, Mother of loves,
A signal from whom excites time to
Confused outbursts, filling spaces with
Lights and leaves. In pelagic meadows
The plankton open their parachutes;
The mountains are amused; mobs of birds
Shout at fat shopkeepers—"Shucks! We are free.
Imitate us"—and out of the blue
Come bright boys with bells on their ankles
To tease with roses Cartesian monks
Till their heads ache, geometers vexed by
Irrelevant reds. May your right hand,
Lightly alighting on their longing flesh,
Promise this pair what their prayers demand,
Bliss in both, born of each other, a
Double dearness; let their dreams descend
Into concrete conduct. Claim your own.

ROSETTA and EMBLE had stopped dancing and sat down on the couch. Now he put his arm around her and said:

Enter my aim from all directions, O
Special spirit whose expressions are
My carnal care, my consolation:
Be many or one. Meet me by chance on

Credulous coasts where cults intersect
Or join as arranged by the Giants' Graves,
Titanic tombs which at twilight bring
Greetings from the great misguided dead;
Hide from, haunt me, on hills to be seen
Far away through the forelegs of mares;
Stay till I come in the startling light
When the tunnel turns to teach surprise,
Or face me and fight for a final stand
With a brave blade in your buffer states,
My visible verb, my very dear,
Till I die, darling.

ROSETTA laid her head on his shoulder and said:
                              O the deep roots
Of the cross-roads yew, calm for so long,
Have felt you afar and faintly begin
To tingle now. What twitters there'll be in
The brook bushes at the bright sound of
Your bicycle bell. What barking then
As you stride the stiles to startle one
Great cry in the kitchen when you come home,
My doom, my darling.

They kissed. Then EMBLE said:
                              Till death divide
May the Four Faces Feeling can make
Assent to our sighs.

She said:
                              The snap of the Three
Grim Spinning Sisters' Spectacle Case
Uphold our honors.

He said:

> The Heavenly Twins
> Guard our togetherness from ghostly ills.

She said:

> The Outer Owner, that Oldest One whom
> This world is with, be witness to our vows.

Which vows they now alternately swore.

> If you blush, I'll build breakwaters.
> When you're tired, I'll tidy your table.
> If you cry, I'll climb crags.
> When you're sick, I'll sit at your side.
> If you frown, I'll fence fields.
> When you're ashamed, I'll shine your shoes.
> If you laugh, I'll liberate lands.
> When you're depressed, I'll play you the piano.
> If you sigh, I'll sack cities.
> When you're unlucky, I'll launder your linen.
> If you sing, I'll save souls.
> When you're hurt, I'll hold your hand.
> If you smile, I'll smelt silver.
> When you're afraid, I'll fetch you food.
> If you talk, I'll track down trolls.
> When you're on edge, I'll empty your ash-tray.
> If you whisper, I'll wage wars.
> When you're cross, I'll clean your coat.
> If you whistle, I'll water wastes.
> When you're bored, I'll bathe your brows.

Again they embraced. QUANT poured out the dregs of the glass on the carpet as a libation and invoked the local spirits:

Ye little larvae, lords of the household,
Potty, P-P, Peppermill, Lampshade,
Funnybone, Faucet, Face-in-the-wall,
Head-over-heels and Upsy-daisy
And Collywobbles and Cupboard-Love,
Be good, little gods, and guard these lives,
Innocent be all your indiscretions,
That no paranoic notion obsess
Nor dazing dump bedevil their minds
With faceless fears; no filter-passing
Virus invade; no invisible germ,
Transgressing rash or gadding tumor
Attack their tissues; nor, taking by
Spiteful surprise, conspiring objects
With slip or sharpness or sly fracture
Menace or mangle the morbid flesh
Of our king and queen.

Now, turning to ROSETTA, MALIN said:
                         O clear Princess,
Learn from your hero his love of play,
Cherish his childishness, choose in him
Your task and toy, your betrayer also
Who gives gladly but forgets as soon
What and why, for the world he is true to
Is his own creation; to act like father,
And beget like God a gayer echo,
An unserious self, is the sole thought
Of this bragging boy. Be to him always
The mother-moment which makes him dream
He is lord of time. Belong to his journey:
O rest on his rock in your red dress,
His youth and future.

Then, turning to EMBLE, he said:

And you, bright Prince,
Invent your steps, go variously about
Her pleasant places, disposed to joy;
O stiffly stand, a staid monadnock,
On her peneplain; placidly graze
On her outwash apron, her own steed;
Dance, a wild deer, in her dark thickets;
Run, a river, all relish through her vales.

Alcohol, lust, fatigue, and the longing to be good, had by now in-
duced in them all a euphoric state in which it seemed as if it were only
some trifling and easily rectifiable error, improper diet, inadequate
schooling, or an outmoded moral code which was keeping mankind
from the millennial Earthly Paradise. Just a little more effort, perhaps
merely the discovery of the right terms in which to describe it, and surely
absolute pleasure must immediately descend upon the astonished
armies of this world and abolish for ever all their hate and suffering. So,
such efforts as at that moment they could, they made. ROSETTA cried:

Let brazen bands abrupt their din and
Song grow civil, for the siege is raised.
The mad gym-mistress, made to resign,
Can pinch no more.

EMBLE cried:

Deprived of their files,
The vice-squads cavort in the mountains,
The Visa-Division vouch for all.

Then ROSETTA:

The shops which displayed shining weapons
And crime-stories carry delicate
Pastoral poems and porcelain groups.

Then EMBLE:

    Nor money, magic, nor martial law,
    Hardness of heart nor hocus-pocus
    Are needed now on the novel earth.

ROSETTA:

    Nor terrors, tides, contagion longer
    Lustrate her stables: their strictures yield
    To play and peace.

EMBLE:

               Where pampered opulent
    Grudges governed, the Graces shall dance
    In excellent order with hands linked.

ROSETTA:

    Where, cold and cruel, critical faces
    Watched from windows, shall wanton putti
    Loose floods of flowers.

EMBLE:

               Where frontier sentries
    Stood so glumly on guard, young girls shall pass
    Trespassing in extravagant clothes.

ROSETTA:

    Where plains winced as punishing engines
    Raised woeful welts, tall windmills shall pat
    The flexible air and fan good cows.

EMBLE:

    Where hunted hundreds helplessly drowned,
    Rose-cheeked riders shall rein their horses
    To smile at swans.

The others joined in chorus. MALIN cried:

It is safe to endure:
Each flat defect has found its solid
Gift to shadow, each goal its unique
Longing to lure, relatedness its
Invariant base, since Venus has now
Agreed so gladly to guarantee
Plenty of water to the plants this year,
Aid to the beasts, to all human demands
Full satisfaction with fresh structures
For crucial regions.

QUANT cried:

A kind word and
A fatherly peak not far away
For city orphans.

Then ROSETTA again:

Synchronized watches
And a long lane with a lot of twists
For both sexes.

And EMBLE:

Barns and shrubberies
For game-playing gangs.

QUANT:

Grates full of logs and
Hinterland homes for old proconsuls
And pensioned pairs.

EMBLE:

Places of silence
For real readers.

ROSETTA:

> A room with a view
> For a shut-in soul.

MALIN:

> A shady walk
> There and back for a thinker or two.

EMBLE:

> A gentle jaunt for dejected nerves
> Over warm waters.

ROSETTA:

> A wild party
> Every night for the outgoing classes.

MALIN:

> A long soliloquy to learn by heart
> For the verbal type.

QUANT:

> Vast museums
> For the acquisitive kind to keep tidy.

MALIN:

> Spigots to open for the spendthrift lot,
> And choke-pear choices for champion wills.

MALIN caught QUANT's eye and they rose to take their leave. As they were getting their hats and coats, QUANT sang:

> O gifted ghosts, be gone now to affirm
> Your dedication; dwell in your choice:
> Venus with grace preventing
> Requires what she may quicken.

Royal with roses be your resting place,
Balmy the airways, blue the welkin that
    Attend your time of passage,
    And easy seas assist you.

MALIN sang:

    Redeem with a clear
    Configuration
    Of routes and goals
    The ages of anguish,
    All griefs endured
    At the feet of appalling
    Fortresses; may
    Your present motions
    Satisfy all
    Their antecedents.

ROSETTA went with them to the elevator. As they waited in the corridor for it to come up, QUANT went on singing:

Wonder warm you with its wisdom now,
Genial joy rejuvenate your days,
    A light of self-translation,
    A blessed interior brightness,

Animate also your object world
Till its pure profiles appear again,
    Losing their latter vagueness,
    In the sharp shapes of childhood.

So did MALIN as they entered the elevator:

    Plumed and potent
    Go forth, fulfil

A happy future
And occupy that
Permanent kingdom
Parameters rule,
Loved by infinite
Populations
Of possible cases:
Away. Farewell.

Then they sank from her sight. When she got back to her apartment, she found that EMBLE had gone into her bedroom and passed out. She looked down at him, half sadly, half relieved, and thought thus:

Blind on the bride-bed, the bridegroom snores,
Too aloof to love. Did you lose your nerve
And cloud your conscience because I wasn't
Your dish really? You danced so bravely
Till I wished I were. Will you remain
Such a pleasant prince? Probably not.
But you're handsome, aren't you? even now
A kingly corpse. I'll coffin you up till
You rule again. Rest for us both and
Dream, dear one. I'll be dressed when you wake
To get coffee. You'll be glad you didn't
While your headache lasts, and I won't shine,
In the sobering sun. We're so apart
When our ways have crossed and our words touched
On Babylon's banks. You'll build here, be
Satisfied soon, while I sit waiting
On my light luggage to leave if called
For some new exile, with enough clothes
But no merry maypole. Make your home
With some glowing girl; forget with her what

Happens also. If ever you see
A fuss forming in the far distance,
Lots of police, and a little group
In terrible trouble, don't try to help;
They'd make you mock and you might be ashamed.
As long as you live may your lying be
Poetic only. I'd hate you to think
How gentile you feel when you join in
The rowdy cries at Rimmon's party:
"—Fasten your figleaf, the Fleet is in.
Caesar is sitting in solemn thought,
Do not disturb. I'm dying tonight with
The tragic poets—" for you'll trust them all,
Be at home in there where a host of creatures,
Shot or squashed, have insured good-luck to
Their bandit bodies, blond mausoleums
Of the inner life. How could I share their
Light elations who belong after
Such hopes end? So be off to the game, dear,
And meet your mischief. I'll mind the shop.
You'll never notice what's not for sale
To charming children. Don't choose to ask me.
You're too late to believe. Your lie is showing,
Your creed is creased. But have Christian luck.
Your Jesus has wept; you may joke now,
Be spick and span, spell out the bumptious
Morals on monuments, mind your poise
And take up your cues, attract Who's-Who,
Ignore What's-Not. Niceness is all and
The rest bores. I'm too rude a question.
You'd learn to loathe, your legs forget their
Store of proverbs, the staircase wit of
The sleep-walker. You'd slip and blame me

When you came to, and couldn't accept
Our anxious hope with no household god or
Harpist's Haven for hearty climbers.
So fluke through unflustered with full marks in
House-geography: let history be.
Time is our trade, to be tense our gift
Whose woe is our weight; for we are His Chosen,
His ragged remnant with our ripe flesh
And our hats on, sent out of the room
By their dying grandees and doleful slaves,
Kicked in corridors and cold-shouldered
At toll-bridges, teased upon the stage,
Snubbed at sea, to seep through boundaries,
Diffuse like firearms through frightened lands,
Transpose our plight like a poignant theme
Into twenty tongues, time-tormented
But His People still. We'll point for Him,
Be as obvious always if He won't show
To threaten their thinking in their way,
Nor His strong arm that stood no nonsense,
Fly, let's face it, to defend us now
When we bruised or broiled our bodies are chucked
Like cracked crocks onto kitchen middens
In the time He takes. We'll trust. He'll slay
If His Wisdom will. He won't alter
Nor fake one fact. Though I fly to Wall Street
Or Publisher's Row, or pass out, or
Submerge in music, or marry well,
Marooned on riches, He'll be right there
With His Eye upon me. Should I hide away
My secret sins in consulting rooms,
My fears are before Him; He'll find all,
Ignore nothing. He'll never let me

Conceal from Him the semi-detached
Brick villa in Laburnum Crescent,
The poky parlor, the pink bows on
The landing-curtains, or the lawn-mower
That wouldn't work, for He won't pretend to
Forget how I began, nor grant belief
In the mythical scenes I make up
Of a home like theirs, the Innocent Place where
His Law can't look, the leaves are so thick.
I've made their magic but their Momma Earth
Is His stone still, and their stately groves,
Though I wished to worship, His wood to me.
More boys like this one may embrace me yet
I shan't find shelter, I shan't be at peace
Till I really take your restless hands,
My poor fat father. How appalling was
Your taste in ties. How you tried to have fun,
You so longed to be liked. You lied so,
Didn't you, dad? When the doll never came,
When mother was sick and the maid laughed.
—Yes, I heard you in the attic. At her grave you
Wept and wilted. Was that why you chose
So blatant a voice, such button eyes
To play house with you then? Did you ever love
Stepmother Stupid? You'd a strange look,
Sad as the sea, when she searched your clothes.
Don't be cruel and cry. I couldn't stay to
Be your baby. We both were asking
For a warmth there wasn't, and then wouldn't write.
We mustn't, must we? Moses will scold if
We're not all there for the next meeting
At some brackish well or broken arch,
Tired as we are. We must try to get on

Though mobs run amok and markets fall,
Though lights burn late at police stations,
Though passports expire and ports are watched,
Though thousands tumble. Must their blue glare
Outlast the lions? Who'll be left to see it
Disconcerted? I'll be dumb before
The barracks burn and boisterous Pharaoh
Grow ashamed and shy. *Shema' Yisra'el:*
'adonai 'elohenu, 'adonai 'echad.

PART SIX

Epilogue

Some natural tears they drop'd, but wip'd them soon;
The world was all before them, where to choose . . .

JOHN MILTON *Paradise Lost*

Meanwhile in the street outside, QUANT and MALIN, after expressing their mutual pleasure at having met, after exchanging addresses and promising to look each other up some time, had parted and immediately forgotten each other's existence. Now MALIN was travelling southward by subway while QUANT was walking eastward, each to his own place. Dawn had begun to break.

Walking through the streets, QUANT sang to himself an impromptu ballad:

> When the Victory Powers convened at Byzantium,
> The shiners declined to show their faces,
> And the ambiences of heaven uttered a plethora
> Of admonitory monsters which dismayed the illiterate.

Sitting in the train, MALIN thought:

> Age softens the sense of defeat
> As well as the will to success,
> Till the unchangeable losses of childhood,
> The forbidden affections rebel
> No more; so now in the mornings
> I wake, neither warned nor refreshed,
> From dreams without daring, a series

Of vaguely disquieting adventures
Which never end in horror,
Grief or forgiving embraces.

QUANT sang:

But peace was promised by the public hepatoscopists
As the Ministers met to remodel the Commonwealth
In what was formerly the Museum of Fashion and Handicrafts,
While husky spectres haunted the corridors.

MALIN thought:

Do we learn from the past? The police,
The dress-designers, etc.,
Who manage the mirrors, say—No.
A hundred centuries hence
The gross and aggressive will still
Be putting their trust in a patron
Saint or a family fortress,
The seedy be taking the same
Old treatments for tedium vitae,
Religion, Politics, Love.

QUANT sang:

The Laurentian Landshield was ruthlessly gerrymandered,
And there was a terrible tussle over the Tethys Ocean;
Commentators broadcast by the courtesy of a shaving-cream
Blow by blow the whole debate on the Peninsulas.

MALIN thought:

Both professor and prophet depress,
For vision and longer view
Agree in predicting a day
Of convulsion and vast evil,
When the Cold Societies clash

Or the mosses are set in motion
To overrun the earth,
And the great brain which began
With lucid dialectics
Ends in horrid madness.

QUANT sang:

But there were some sensible settlements in the sub-committees:
The Duodecimal System was adopted unanimously,
The price of obsidian pegged for a decade,
Technicians sent north to get nitrogen from the ice-cap.

MALIN thought:

Yet the noble despair of the poets
Is nothing of the sort; it is silly
To refuse the tasks of time
And, overlooking our lives,
Cry—"Miserable wicked me,
How interesting I am."
We would rather be ruined than changed,
We would rather die in our dread
Than climb the cross of the moment
And let our illusions die.

QUANT sang:

Outside these decisions the cycle of Nature
Revolved as usual, and voluble sages
Preached from park-benches to passing fornicators
A Confucian faith in the Functional Society.

MALIN thought:

We're quite in the dark: we do not
Know the connection between
The clock we are bound to obey

And the miracle we must not despair of;
We simply cannot conceive
With any feelings we have
How the raging lion is to lime
With the yearning unicorn;
Nor shall we, till total shipwreck
Deprive us of our persons.

QUANT had now reached the house where he lived and, as he started to climb the steps of his stoop, he tripped and almost fell. At which he said:

Why, Miss *ME*, what's the matter? *Must* you go woolgathering?
Once I was your wonder. How short-winded you've gotten.
Come, Tinklebell, trot. Let's pretend you're a thoroughbred.
Over the hill now into Abraham's Bosom.

So saying, he opened his front door and disappeared. But MALIN's journey was still not done. He was thinking:

For the new locus is never
Hidden inside the old one
Where Reason could rout it out,
Nor guarded by dragons in distant
Mountains where Imagination
Could explore it; the place of birth
Is too obvious and near to notice,
Some dull dogpatch a stone's throw
Outside the walls, reserved
For the eyes of faith to find.

Now the train came out onto the Manhattan Bridge. The sun had risen. The East River glittered. It would be a bright clear day for work and for war.

MALIN thought:

> For the others, like me, there is only the flash
> Of negative knowledge, the night when, drunk, one
> Staggers to the bathroom and stares in the glass
> To meet one's madness, when what mother said seems
> Such darling rubbish and the decent advice
> Of the liberal weeklies as lost an art
> As peasant pottery, for plainly it is not
> To the Cross or to *Clarté* or to Common Sense
> Our passions pray but to primitive totems
> As absurd as they are savage; science or no science,
> It is Bacchus or the Great Boyg or Baal-Peor,
> Fortune's Ferris-wheel or the physical sound
> Of our own names which they actually adore as their
> Ground and goal. Yet the grossest of our dreams is
> No worse than our worship which for the most part
> Is so much galimatias to get out of
> Knowing our neighbor, all the needs and conceits of
> The poor muddled maddened mundane animal
> Who is hostess to us all, for each contributes his
> Personal panic, his predatory note
> To her gregarious grunt as she gropes in the dark
> For her lost lollypop. We belong to our kind,
> Are judged as we judge, for all gestures of time
> And all species of space respond in our own
> Contradictory dialect, the double talk
> Of ambiguous bodies, born like us to that
> Natural neighborhood which denial itself
> Like a friend confirms; they reflect our status,
> Temporals pleading for eternal life with
> The infinite impetus of anxious spirits,
> Finite in fact yet refusing to be real,
> Wanting our own way, unwilling to say Yes
> To the Self-So which is the same at all times,

That Always-Opposite which is the whole subject
Of our not-knowing, yet from no necessity
Condescended to exist and to suffer death
And, scorned on a scaffold, ensconced in His life
The human household. In our anguish we struggle
To elude Him, to lie to Him, yet His love observes
His appalling promise; His predilection
As we wander and weep is with us to the end,
Minding our meanings, our least matter dear to Him,
His Good ingressant on our gross occasions
Envisages our advance, valuing for us
Though our bodies too blind or too bored to examine
What sort excite them are slain interjecting
Their childish Ows and, in choosing how many
And how much they will love, our minds insist on
Their own disorder as their own punishment,
His Question disqualifies our quick senses,
His Truth makes our theories historical sins,
It is where we are wounded that is when He speaks
Our creaturely cry, concluding His children
In their mad unbelief to have mercy on them all
As they wait unawares for His World to come.

So thinking, he returned to duty reclaimed by the actual world
where time is real and in which, therefore, poetry can take no interest.

Facing another long day of servitude to wilful authority and blind
accident, creation lay in pain and earnest, once more reprieved from
self-destruction, its adoption, as usual, postponed.

APPENDIX

Two Letters on Metrical Matters

In 1952 Alan Ward, a medievalist at Wadham College, Oxford, wrote to Auden about Anglo-Saxon meters in *The Age of Anxiety*. Ward was preparing a course of lectures on alliterative verse and thought that it would be interesting to conclude with a reference to Auden's demonstration that these ancient traditions still had much poetic life in them. Auden replied from Ischia, an island in the Bay of Naples, where he lived for part of each year from 1948 to 1957:

Aug 30
Via Santa Lucia 14
Forio d'Ischia
Prov. di Napoli

Dear Mr. Ward,

Thank you for your letter of Aug 25 inquiring about the metre of The Age of Anxiety.

1) I made some attempts to obey the quantity rules of O.E. but abandoned them; as in all quantitative experiments in modern English so many vowels become long by position that, without an obviously artificial diction, you cannot get enough Lifts of the Accented-Short-unaccented-short type.

2) To compensate for this relaxation, I took from the romance tradition syllabic counting. In the first two parts of the poem, for instance, the number of syllables in the whole line is 9, so that the caesura always divides asymmetrically. There is one 2:7 line, I believe, but most are 5:4, 4:5, 3:6, 6:3 etc. Contiguous vowels and vowels through h elide. In the more lyrical sections, I have allowed myself more freedom, and, as I expect you will have seen, in many places I have imitated or

modified Icelandic meters. I have tried also to follow O.E. practice in avoiding a dactylic rhythm and in ending sentences in the mid-line.

3) The alliteration conforms, I hope, to O.E. rules.

I hope this answers your questions. If you want to know anything more, my address after Sept 14 is 235 Seventh Avenue, New York City 11.

yours sincerely

W. H. Auden

After a follow-up query from Ward, which has survived only in partial draft, Auden wrote again:

Dec 28

235 Seventh Avenue

New York City 11

New York

U.S.A.

Dear Mr Ward,

Thank you for your letter of Dec 22. In answer to your first question, I originally started out with the intention of writing a poem of forty or fifty lines, but, once I began, the metre seemed to offer so many possibilities that I changed my mind and wrote a long poem.

There are lines in which the second alliteration is not exact, but I believe or hope that the first and third are always correct, eg

st. s. st. x

Occasionally the same alliteration is used in consecutive lines, but I don't think there is a case of linked alliteration. Cross alliteration is only used in some of the lyrical bits, eg p 61 (Lights are moving) and p 68 (These ancient harbors).

Quite a lot of The Seven Stages is written in Ljoðuháttr, and the lyric on p 39 (Deep in my dark the dream shines) is in Kviðuháttr. P 104 (Hushed is the lake of hawks) is an attempt at a Drápa.

As C. S. Lewis has pointed out, one of the values of the O.E. metre is that it naturally accepts the spondee in a way that our normal 'french' metric does not. On the whole, I suspect that it is a metre which is only suitable to rather sombre subjects, but I may be wrong.

with best wishes for the success of your lectures

yours sincerely,
W. H. Auden

The poems Auden mentions may be found in this edition as follows:

"Lights are moving," 49
"These ancient harbors," 56
"Deep in my dark the dream shines," 30
"Hushed is the lake of hawks," 88

The reference to C. S. Lewis indicates his essay "A Metrical Suggestion" (*Lysistrata* 2:1, May 1935), later several times reprinted under the title "The Alliterative Metre"—for example, in *Rehabilitations and Other Essays*, ed. Walter Hooper (London: Oxford University Press, 1939). Auden told Alan Ansen that "C. S. Lewis is really the best man I've seen on alliterative." Auden's short poem "Seen when night was silent" appeared in the same issue of *Lysistrata*, so it seems likely that he encountered Lewis's article in that venue.

These letters are especially valuable as evidence of Auden's mature understanding of poetic technique. The changes to his early poetry that he made when he began collecting his verse—his first *Collected Poems* appeared in 1945—are notorious, and it is usually assumed that his alterations were prompted by his move to Christianity. Sometimes this is true, but often Auden was frustrated by what he believed to be his earlier technical errors.

An account of this correspondence, entitled "Two New Letters by Auden on Anglo-Saxon Metre and *The Age of Anxiety*," by Jane Toswell and Alan Ward, may be found in *The Year's Work in Medievalism* XV, edited by Gwendolyn Morgan (Bozeman, MT: Studies in Medievalism, 2000), 57–73.

TEXTUAL NOTES

ABBREVIATIONS

Berg   The Henry W. and Albert A. Berg Collection of English and American Literature at the New York Public Library.

CP   Auden, *Collected Poems*, ed. Edward Mendelson (New York: Modern Library, 2007).

CSP   Auden, *Collected Shorter Poems: 1927–1957* (London: Faber & Faber, 1966).

DH   Auden, *The Dyer's Hand and Other Essays* (New York: Random House,1962).

HUA   Harvard University Archives

JF   John Fuller, *W. H. Auden: A Commentary* (Princeton: Princeton University Press, 1998).

LA   Edward Mendelson, *Later Auden* (New York: Farrar, Strauss and Giroux, 1999).

PP   Alan Myers and Robert Forsythe, *W. H. Auden: Pennine Poet* (Nenthead, Cumbria: North Pennines Heritage Trust, 1999).

P1   *The Complete Works of W. H. Auden: Prose and Travel Books in Verse: Volume I: 1926–1938*, ed. Edward Mendelson (Princeton: Princeton University Press, 1996).

P2   *The Complete Works of W. H. Auden: Prose: Volume II: 1939–1948*, ed. Edward Mendelson (Princeton: Princeton University Press, 2002).

P3   *The Complete Works of W. H. Auden: Prose: Volume III: 1949–1955*, ed. Edward Mendelson (Princeton: Princeton University Press, 2008).

SP   Auden, *Selected Poems*, expanded edition, ed. Edward Mendelson (New York: Vintage, 2007).

TT   Alan Ansen, *The Table Talk of W. H. Auden* (London: Faber & Faber, 1990).

In the notes that follow, the Bible is cited from the Authorized (King James) Version, since that is the one that Auden knew and used. Definitions of unusual words are adapted from the first edition of the *Oxford English Dictionary*: by the time he wrote *The Age of Anxiety* Auden had acquired a complete set of the *OED* and was deeply devoted to it—*too* devoted, think some who have had to navigate the more recondite areas of his vocabulary.

Much information about the textual history of this poem and the parts thereof—as given in these notes and in the portion of the Introduction devoted to the text of this edition—is taken from *W. H. Auden: a Bibliography, 1924–1969*, 2nd ed., ed. B. C. Bloomfield and Edward Mendelson (Charlottesville: University Press of Virginia, 1972).

PREFACE

Page

vii "I sit in one": SP 95.

vii "a bar on Third Avenue": See page 19 below.

vii "In war-time": See page 3 below.

viii "One fine summer night": "The Protestant Mystics," in *Auden's Forewords and Afterwords* (New York: Random House, 1973), 69.

viii "Out on the lawn": SP 30.

INTRODUCTION

Page

xi "It's frightfully long": *TT* 8.

xi "J.R.R. Tolkien's lectures": "I remember [a lecture] I attended, delivered by Professor Tolkien. I do not remember a single word he said but at a certain point he recited, and magnificently, a long passage of *Beowulf*. I was spellbound. This poetry, I knew, was going to be my dish. I became willing, therefore, to work at Anglo-Saxon because, unless I did, I should never be able to read this poetry. I learned enough to read it, however sloppily, and Anglo-Saxon and Middle English poetry have been one of my strongest, most lasting influences." From Auden's inaugural lecture as Professor of Poetry at Oxford University in 1956 (*DH* 41–42).

xii "I shall, I hope": Letter to Theodore Spencer, 16 April 1939, *HUA*.

xiii "I should have got along": *TT* 47.

xiii "I keep wishing": Letter to Elizabeth Mayer, 9 May 1945 (cited in *LA* 284).

xiii "the fact of the Nazis' genocidal murder": So claims Edward Mendelson, *LA* 257n.

xiii "The Shakespeare course": Letter to Theodore Spencer, 10 February 1946, *HUA*.

xiii "I was still too young": *CSP* 15.

xiv "Hamlet": Act 3, scene 2.

xiv "You go not": Act 3, scene 4.

xiv "My deuce, my double": See page 6 below.

xiv "Every child": *P2* 161.

xv "It's as if": *CP* 352.

xv "The police, / The dress-designers": See page 104 below.

xv "Hannah Arendt": See the preface to *Between Past and Future* (New York: Viking, 1968 [1954]

xvi "Let Ares doze, that other war": *CP* 334–37.

xvi "But the new barbarian": See page 16 below.

xvii "Lies and lethargies": See page 17 below.

xvii "Quant points a finger": See page 21 below.

xviii "Psychoanalysis, like all": *P2* 162. Auden offers a shortened and somewhat toned-down version of this essay in the section of *The Dyer's Hand* called "Hic et Ille" (94). "The last state of that man was worse than the first" quotes Matthew 12:45.

xviii "this doctor": *CP* 271.

xix "*Psychologische Typen*": See *Psychological Types,* The Collected Works of C. G. Jung, vol. 6, trans. H. G. Baynes, rev. R.F.C. Hull, Bollingen Series, 20 (Princeton: Princeton University Press, 1971).

xix "The Four Faculties": *CP* 355.

xx "Bosh, straight from Jung": See *LA* 247.

xxi "That catastrophic situation": *SP* 130. When Auden prepared the 1945 *Collected Poems*, probably in 1942, he edited out this stanza, along with several others.

xxii "When I was delivering": *TT* 11.

xxii "From Seager's Folly": See page 7 below.

xxii "won't pretend to": See page 101 below.

xxiii "favorite day-dream": See page 5 below.

xxiii "if I have any work": "The Guilty Vicarage" *P2* 261–70. This essay was written in early 1946 and published in *Harper's* (May 1948). Also, in 1936 Auden published a poem called "Detective Story," which concludes with these lines: "But time is always guilty. Someone must pay for / Our loss of happiness, our happiness itself" (*CP* 152).

xxiii "A crime has occurred": See page 15 below.

xxiv "The murder": Notebook in the Poetry Library at the State University of New York at Buffalo; cited in *LA* 246.

xxiv "topophilia": *P2* 306.

xxiv "Betjeman is really the only person": *TT* 25, 60.

xxv "Betjeman is really a minor poet": *TT* 60.

xxv "may our luck find": See page 46 below. In "The Sea and the Mirror" Caliban offers a contemptuous parody of the Arcadian hope: "Carry me back, Master, to the cathedral town where the canons run through the water meadows with butterfly nets and the old women keep sweetshops in the cobbled side streets. . . . Give me my passage home, let me see that harbour once again just as it was before I learned the bad words. . . . Look, Uncle, look. They have broken my glasses and I have lost my silver whistle. Pick me up, Uncle, let little Johnny ride away on your massive shoulders to recover his green kingdom . . ." (*CP* 436).

xxv "Thinking-Intuitive type": Letter to Spender of 13 March 1941 (Berg); cited in *LA* 165. In an essay on the poetry of Thomas Hardy published a year earlier, Auden had written, "I, like my mother, was a thinking-intuitive" (*P2* 44).

xxv "John Thompson": Professor Paul Weindling, the author of a forthcoming biography of John Thompson (*John W. Thompson: Psychiatrist in the Shadow of the Holocaust* [Rochester, NY: University of Rochester Press, 2010]) has a copy of *The Age of Anxiety* that Auden had inscribed to Thompson. It reads,

> To Malin
> with love
> from
> The Bartender
> Dec 1947

xxvi "Orthodoxy is reticence": Auden uses this phrase often: see *DH* 21, *Forewords and Afterwords* 71, and *The Viking Book of Aphorisms*, which Auden coedited with Louis Kronenberger (1962). In also turns up in slightly different form in "'The Truest Poetry is the Most Feigning'" (*CP* 617). In the anthology the phrase is attributed to "Anonymous," but elsewhere Auden credits it to an unnamed bishop. Given that Auden in later life often reflected that if he had taken holy orders he would have become a bishop, I am tempted to think that he coined the phrase himself; but Edward Mendelson suggests that it may have emerged from a conversation with the historian Edgar Wind (*LA* 369).

xxvi "this season, the man": *P2* 307.

xxvi "Why, Miss *ME*": See page 106 below.

xxvii "Consider . . . the incessant": See page 20 below.

xxvii "the famous speech by Jaques": Act 2, scene 7.

xxvii "Behold the infant": See page 23 below.

xxvii "His last chapter": See page 42 below.

xxviii "O show us the route": See page 45 below.

xxviii "So it was now": See page 46 below.

xxviii "the shape of the Edenic quest": *LA* 250.

xxix "really quite straightforward": From Alan Ansen's diary (Berg); see *LA* 251.

xxix "the Zohar": Auden used the five-volume English edition edited by Harry Sperling and Maurice Simon (London: Soncino Press, 1931).

xxix "*paysage moralisé*": The poem of that title (*CP* 119)—though written a dozen years earlier, before Auden knew anything of Jung, and when he had no thought of becoming a Christian—looks strangely like a summary or condensation of "The Seven Stages." Auden would pursue some of its themes in the early fifties in a sequence of poems called "Bucolics," but his greatest achievement in the *paysage moralisé* tradition is a poem he wrote soon after completing *The Age of Anxiety*, "In Praise of Limestone."

xxix "Dream Quest": *P2* 283. See also Auden's 1940 poetic sequence "The Quest" as a kind of first approach to the quest story (*CP* 283–93).

xxx "tacit tarn": See page 47 below.

xxx "a common goal": See page 57 below.

xxx "our common hope": See page 52 below.

xxxi "as they run": See page 64 below.

xxxi "the temptation to sin": *P2* 134.

xxxi "universal democracy": Auden learned about All Souls' Day from *Out of Revolution: Autobiography of Western Man* (1938), a massive work by the eccentric Christian philosopher/historian Eugen Rosenstock-Huessy. For many years Auden adapted Rosenstock-Huessy's historical theories and wrote in 1970 that he had "read everything by him that I could lay my hands on" (foreword to *I Am an Impure Thinker* [Norwich, VT, Argo Books [1970)], i).

xxxi "vanish down solitary": See page 72 below.

xxxi "Their journey has been": See page 78 below.

xxxii "some semi-divine stranger": See page 83 below.

xxxii "In times of war": See page 88 below.

xxxii "the millennial Earthly Paradise": See page 93 below.

xxxii "Eros, builder of cities": *CP* 274.

xxxiii "a little altar": See page 89 below.

xxxiii "to devise a rhetoric": Letter to Theodore Spencer, 16 December 1946, *HUA*.

xxxiii "so speaks comically": *DH* 145.

xxxiii "Reluctantly, I agree": Letter of 16 December 1946, *HUA*.

xxxiv "Ronald Firbank and an Amateur World": This was delivered as a radio talk on the BBC Third Programme, 29 April 1961, and printed in the *Listener*'s issue of 8 June.

xxxiv "QUANT and MALIN": See page 103 below.

xxxiv "The term 'individual'": *P2* 308.

xxxv "The difference between": *P2* 171.

xxxvi "Though I fly": See page 100 below.

xxxvi "defence against": Letter to Theodore Spencer, 16 December 1946, *HUA*.

xxxvi "In our anguish": See page 108 below.

xxxvii "the greatest grandest opera": *CP* 441.

xxxviii "conscious theatrical exaggeration": From Auden's inaugural lecture as Oxford's Professor of Poetry in 1956 (reprinted in *DH* 48).

xxxviii *"Sir Gawain and the Green Knight"*: Auden told Alan Ansen that *Pearl*— another poem by this anonymous genius—"is a great rhymed alliterative poem" (*TT* 54).

xxxix "Auden complained": "You know, for three years, I had to eat lunch every day with a horrible jukebox blaring away. It was in a drug store in Swarthmore. There was no other place to eat. I thought I'd go out of my mind if I heard 'I'm Dreaming of a White Christmas' one more time. And did you know that little ditty 'There'll Be a Hot Time in the Town of Berlin'? That reached peaks of popularity in 1944, but it stopped abruptly about the time the Battle of the Bulge began. The jukebox is really an invention straight out of hell" (*TT* 40).

xxxix "For better or worse": *P2* 307.

xxxix "one / Staggers to": See page 107 below.

xl "a planetary visitor": From Auden's untitled contribution to a book of essays called *Modern Canterbury Pilgrims* (*P3* 579).

xl "Auden's efforts to": *LA* 251.

xli "Jacques Barzun's commendation": In *Harper's* (September 1947) Barzun praised the poem extravagantly, noting that "the very title . . . roots it in our generation."

   Time's unsigned article (21 July 1947), which in the magazine's parlance of the period describes its subject as "Poet Auden," claims that "The Age of Anxiety is the best knit of Auden's longer works; his Bright Ideas, which have always had a way of stealing the show, this time wait for their cues. For the first time, too, Auden has created characters who are not only types but individuals." And it concludes with this comment: "On one wall of his littered study Poet Auden keeps an immense map of Alston moor in Cumberland below the Roman Wall, his childhood country, whose limestone quarries, fells and valleys—and mining machinery—have persisted as bleakly beautiful imagery in all his work."

xli "Leonard Bernstein's": Much of the information in this paragraph is taken from *W. H. Auden: A Bibliography: 1924–1969*, 2nd ed., ed. B. C. Bloomfield and Edward Mendelson (Charlottesville: University Press of Virginia, 1972), 61. The claim that Auden disliked the Bernstein-Robbins ballet is made by Lincoln Kirstein, who was general director of the ballet at that time (*Thirty Years: Lincoln Kirstein's The New York City Ballet* [New York: Alfred A. Knopf, 1978], 76).

xli "Theatre Intime": The performance text, prepared entirely by the undergraduate group, is in the Princeton University Library.

xli "Now each of us": *CP* 627.

xlii "little earlier material": Manuscript scraps and fragments of the poem will probably continue to come to light; the bookseller Robert A. Wilson's collection (now in the University of Delaware Library) includes a loose page from a notebook with a pencil draft of the brief prose passage that begins "Here the radio, breaking in with its banal noises," and another page with a pencil draft of the closing prose narrative.

xliii "the 'Isherwood text'": This and other quotations dealing with the text of the poem and the blurbs come from the materials that Ansen donated to the Berg.

xliii "Isherwood simply carried": On his way to England in January of 1947, Isherwood's diary notes, he "stayed night of 20th with Wystan." Presumably that's when he returned the manuscript, though he was back in New York in May and stayed through much of June. *Diaries, Volume 1: 1939–1960*, ed. Katherine Bucknell (New York: Harper, 1996), 391–92.

xliv "I'm never going": *TT* 61.

xlviii "In my contract": *TT* 21–22.

xlviii "It isnt that": This quotation, and those that follow, are taken from Nicholas Jenkins's article "'All Types That Can Intrigue the Writer's Fancy,'" in the *W. H. Auden Society Newsletter* 6 (December 1990): http://audensociety.org/06newsletter.html.

THE AGE OF ANXIETY

Page

1 "To John Betjeman": See the Introduction, page xxiv above. On the title page of his typescript in the Berg, Alan Ansen has written this dedication, but then, next to it, "CANCELLED." This may suggest some vacillation

about the dedication. Below that Ansen has written the line from Ronald Firbank that, in the final version, serves as the epigraph to Part Five, but it, too, is marked "CANCELLED." For more on Firbank, see the Introduction, page xxxiii above.

1 "*Lacrimosa dies illa*": The "*Dies Irae*" (Day of Wrath) is a thirteenth-century poem, commonly attributed to Thomas of Celano, a disciple of St. Francis of Assisi. The poem describes the terrors of Judgment Day—the moment at the end of history when all human beings are judged by the returning Christ—and pleads for mercy on that day. The hymn is closely associated with All Souls' Day. The lines cited here come from the penultimate stanza of the hymn and may be roughly translated: "That tearful day, on which accused humanity will rise from the burning coals to be judged." This epigraph is absent from Ansen's typescript in the Berg so was apparently added very late in the process of composition.

PART I: PROLOGUE

3 "*Now the day is over*": Sabine Baring-Gould (1834–1924) was an Anglican priest and a prolific writer in many genres. He is best remembered for his hymns, the most famous of which is "Onward, Christian Soldiers," though "Now the Day Is Over" (1867) was scarcely less popular. Auden's citation of it indicates a genuine affection for Victorian religious expression—a love of everyday Victoriana was a trait he shared with John Betjeman—but of course he also understood that the style had become archaic and twee.

Ansen's typescript in the Berg bears the epigraph, in Ansen's hand,

> "O opportunity, thy guilt is great"
> —Shakespeare, *The Rape of Lucrece*

But this is marked "CANCELLED," and replaced (in Ansen's hand) by the Baring-Gould quatrain. In the typescript none of the six parts of the poem bears an individual epigraph.

3 "When the historical process": Auden seems at one point to have intended to use verse for the descriptive passages, such as this one, that he eventually wrote in prose. A small manuscript notebook formerly in the possession of Robert A. Wilson, now in the University of Delaware Library, has on its title page "The Age of Anxiety | An Eclogue." The next right-hand page contains an abandoned verse opening for the poem, but nothing more from *The Age of Anxiety* except, near the back of the book, some penciled drafts

that may be sketches for "The Dirge." The abandoned opening reads (as transcribed by Edward Mendelson):

> Summer was in the city. Saturday night
> Paraded his riches and unrest before
> The untruthful traveller, whose temporal eye
> Is biassed towards bigness since his body must
> Exaggerate to exist, exhibiting Man
> Acquisitive, unquiet, in quest of his own
> Absconded self. From scarifying newsreels
> Of amphibious forces on foreign beaches
> His guilt looked back at him begrimed and haggard,
> His wilfulness waved as it waited to attack
> Normandy from the north, and the noise of the El
> Was as thankless as his thoughts. On Third Avenue
> As it moved towards midnight, in a modest bar
> Upon high stools, sat an air-force corporal,
> A middle-aged woman, a merchant seaman
> And a vague little man in civilian clothes,
> Each a first acquaintance, four persons [?with] three,
> Growing bolder over beers while the barman watched,
> A vigilant umpire. The civilian spoke.

The odd phrase "four persons with three" seems to mean that each of the four was in the presence of three others.

A separate page in the same collection, detached from one of Auden's large ledger notebooks, has a pencil draft of the opening prose description of the four characters. The character who became Quant has a name in which some of the letters seem to be Cond—y——. Malin is named Marshall, while Rosetta and Emble appear under those names.

3 "happily certain that the one": See these lines from "Out on the lawn": "And when the birds and rising sun / Waken me, I shall speak with one / Who has not gone away" (*SP* 31). See the Preface, page viii above.

4 "a shipping office near the Battery": On the southern tip of Manhattan Island.

4 "More, that is, as": This whole paragraph was added as a typed insert to Ansen's typescript in the Berg.

4 "had had to leave Ireland in a hurry": In a letter to Theodore Spencer (16 December 1946) Auden wrote, "I think of him myself as an Irishman," which suggests that the decision to identify him explicitly as such came late

in the process of writing. Since Malin is Canadian and Rosetta was born in England, Emble is the only native-born American among the four protagonists. This reinforces the notion, introduced three paragraphs previously, that "in war-time . . . everybody is reduced to the anxious status of a shady character or a displaced person."

5 "English detective stories": See the Introduction, page xxiii above.

6 "It was the night of All Souls": See the Introduction, page xxxi above. These words are added, in Ansen's hand, to Ansen's typescript in the Berg so were decided upon very late in the poem's composition.

6 "What flavor has / That liquor": In *The Ambidextrous Universe: Mirror Asymmetry and Time-Reversed Worlds* (New York: Scribner's, 1979 [1964]), Martin Gardner notes that Auden was a lover of Lewis Carroll, and that in the first chapter of *Through the Looking-Glass* (1871) Alice says to her kitten, "How would you like to live in Looking-glass House, Kitty? I wonder if they'd give you milk in there? Perhaps Looking-glass milk isn't good to drink." Gardner also points out that an alcoholic beverage "contains carbon compounds called esters which give it flavor, and most esters are asymmetrical. No one knows what flavor Looking-glass liquor might have, but it is a good bet that it would not taste the same as ordinary liquor unless, of course, it were tasted by a Looking-glass Irishman" (116). See also *JF* 374.

When Auden provided his selection of the best books of 1965 for the *Observer* of London (19 December 1965), he included Gardner's *The Ambidextrous Universe.*

6 "For a soiled soul": Changed in the second Random House printing from "To a soiled soul."

6 "*Schadenfreude*": German, "joy in the misfortune of others."

7 "No chimpanzee / Thinks it thinks": Both of the major notebooks for this poem, at the Beinecke Library at Yale University and the Harry Ransom Center at the University of Texas, indicate that Auden had a great deal of trouble with this speech. There are more crossings-out and revisions for it than for any other verse in the notebooks.

7 "His greenest arcadias": On Arcadianism, see the Introduction, page xxi above.

7 "self-slaughter": The first soliloquy of Hamlet, that prince of anxiety (1.2):

> O, that this too too solid flesh would melt,
> Thaw and resolve itself into a dew!
> Or that the Everlasting had not fix'd
> His canon 'gainst self-slaughter!

7 "Seager's Folly": The name seems to be fictional—as are the names of churches later in the speech—but Robert Forsythe is convinced that the scene described matches quite closely "the view west over [Auden's] York birthplace from the 807 foot high Garrowby Hill" (*PP* 32).

7 "Incisive rains": Ansen's typescript in the Berg reads, "streams."

8 "The malcontented": Ansen's typescript in the Berg reads, "Normal malcontents."

9 "To grasp and gaze": Changed in the second Random House printing from "To grasp and gaze in have got no further."

9 "Their flesh as it felt": Ansen's typescript in the Berg reads, "The flesh as it was."

10 "*Rochester barber / Fools foe*": After this, and before "*Pope condemns*," Ansen's typescript in the Berg has

> Reinforcements rushed
> To pocket by plane. Paratroopers
> Occupy airfield. Allies ignore
> Peace feeler. . .

10 "*Valdivian Deep*": Valdivia is a city on the Chilean coast, and the nearby forests are referred to as Valdivian, but I am not aware of any "Valdivian deep."

10 "Anxious into air": Changed in the second Random House printing from "Anxious into air; instruments glowed."

10 "Not twisting tracks": Changed in the second Random House printing from "Not tricky targets their trigger hands / Are given goals by; we began our run."

10 "Hatched in an instant": Changed in the second Random House printing from "Which instantly hatched."

11 "Why have They killed me?": In 1943 Auden wrote a letter to Elizabeth Mayer in which he related a long talk he had had with John Thompson, the British medical liaison officer on whom the character of Malin would later be modeled: "Thompson was nursing a mortally-wounded gunner in one of the raids over Cologne, who just kept asking, 'Why have They killed me?'" (*LA* 255).

11 "fioritura": In music, an exaggerated flourish or embellishment.

11 "Many have perished; more will": John Fuller hears here an echo of the tenth-century Anglo-Saxon poem "Deor," or "The Lament of Deor," which (unusually for Anglo-Saxon poetry) has a refrain: "Þæs ofereode, þisses swa mæg"—"That passed, so may this."

11 "All war's woes": Ansen's typescript in the Berg reads, "What is war? I can well imagine."

12 "groynes": or "groins": Walls or timber frames built to hold back an encroaching sea.

12 "denes": Wooded valleys.

13 "I see in my mind": It is the Battle of Britain that Rosetta, an English native, thinks of.

13 "Some *miserere*": The Latin *Miserere me, Domine* means "Have mercy on me, Lord."

14 "Four who are famous confer in a *schloss*": *Schloss* is German for "castle." It is not clear that Rosetta has particular historical figures in mind in this passage, though her thoughts would have been prompted by the various conferences and meetings of world leaders that preceded the war and continued through it.

15 "A crime has occurred, accusing all": See the Introduction, page xxiii above. Ansen's typescript in the Berg reads, "A crime has occurred which accuses all," with the final version penciled in.

16 "Tastes and textures": The first printing ends this line with "preferred" and begins the next with "The."

16 "Art to action": This line was mistakenly omitted from the second Random House printing, and not restored until 1968, in the *Collected Longer Poems* (London: Faber & Faber).

16 "But the new barbarian": See the Introduction, page xvi above.

17 "What pain taught": Corrected by Auden on Ansen's typescript in the Berg from "bought"; evidently Ansen's misreading of the manuscript.

17 "farouche": Shy in a sullen way.

17 "the hump of Saturn / Over modest Mimas": In Greek mythology, Mimas is one of the Titans who rebelled against the Olympian gods. He was scalded with hot metal by Hephaestus, and killed by Heracles. But "hump," "Saturn," and "modest" here are impenetrable.

18 "seizin": Legal possession.

18 "our Zion is / A doomed Sodom": Zion, from Mount Zion near Jerusalem, came to stand for the whole land of Israel in its idealized state, the blessed inheritance of God's people. Sodom and Gomorrah are the "cities of the plain" in Genesis 18 and 19 whose gross sins are condemned by God.

18 "all John Doakes and G.I. Joes": John Doakes is a name once used in law, like the more common John Doe, as a pseudonym or a legal fiction, and used more commonly to refer to any ordinary person. Presumably the plural here should be "John Doakeses."

19 "the El on / Third Avenue": The Third Avenue El (elevated train) ran almost the full length of Manhattan, and the bar was perhaps somewhere

along the line in lower or mid-Manhattan, neighborhoods frequented by
Auden in the 1940s.

20 "His pure I / Must give account of and greet his Me": This seems to be a
version of a distinction, dear to Auden, between the active Ego that chooses
and observes and the passive Self that conforms to biological necessity, psy-
chological compulsions, and social conventions. As Edward Mendelson has
rightly noted, "The distinction between ego and self has exasperated virtu-
ally every reader of Auden's prose because he seems to have treated it al-
most as self-explanatory" (*LA* 339n).

20 "this guilt the insoluble": Changed in the second Random House printing
from "this guilt his insoluble."

21 "The Gung-Ho Group . . .": These titles are only partly explicable but are
meant to suggest, ironically, that the four new acquaintances are the sort of
people who would create social organizations devoted to good cheer and
moral improvement. Ganymede was a beautiful young mortal who was ab-
ducted by Zeus to serve as the gods' cupbearer; Auden may also have re-
membered the Junior Ganymede Club frequented by Jeeves and his fellow
valets in the novels of P. G. Wodehouse. "Bide-a-wee" is a Scots phrase
meaning "stay a while." "Sans-souci" means "without care."

21 "*HOMO ABYSSUS OCCIDENTALIS*": By analogy to *Homo sapiens* ("thinking
human"), this coinage identifies Western ("Occidental") humans as crea-
tures of the abyss. Ansen's typescript in the Berg reads "Abyssinia" for "Abys-
sus," an indication of Alan Ansen's struggles to read Auden's handwriting.

PART TWO: THE SEVEN AGES

Page

23 "*A sick toss'd vessel*": These are the final lines of Herbert's poem. Though
Auden sometimes expressed his disapproval of devotional poetry—see, e.g.,
DH 458—he made an exception for the poetry of Herbert (1593–1633). In
the last year of his life he wrote in the introduction to his 1973 selection of
Herbert's poems, "Herbert is a true poet, but a poet *sui generis*, the merits
of whose poems will never be felt without a sympathy with the mind and
character of the man. My own sympathy is unbounded." *George Herbert: Se-
lected by W. H. Auden* (Harmondsworth: Penguin, 1973), xii.

On Ansen's typescript in the Berg this epigraph is written in by Ansen.

23 "Behold the infant": See the Introduction, page xxvii above.

24 "Sank the gas-tanks": "I'm amazed no one here knows what a 'gasometer' is. I wanted to use it for *The Age of Anxiety* and couldn't for that reason. I was heartbroken. I want the poem to be completely American in language" (*TT* 21–22). He had to use "gas-tanks" instead.

26 "He has laid his life-bet": Changed in the second Random House printing from "He has laid his bet with a lying self."

28 "waking, I skipped to": Changed in the second Random House printing from "waking, I stumbled / To the shower."

28 "the hiss of the water": Changed in the second Random House printing from "the hissing of the water."

28 "Since the neighbors did": Auden told Alan Ansen that "the main sources" for this speech "were Baudelaire and Botticelli's *Primavera*" (*TT* 70).

29 "heroic herms": A herm is a statue of Hermes with an erect phallus. These were common in the ancient world.

30 "the Wallomatic": A popular American model of jukebox, made by the Seeburg Corporation of Chicago. Seeburg introduced wall-mounted units for diner booths in 1939, so this was a relatively new technology when the poem was written. Ansen's typescript in the Berg has "juke-box" crossed through and replaced, in Auden's hand, by the misspelled "Wallmatic."

30 "*The Case Is Closed (Tchaikovsky-Fink)*": The notebook in the Ransom Center says "Tschaikovsky-Finkel"; Auden seems to be suggesting a union of (musically) highly wrought Romanticism and (lyrically) Tin Pan Alley. He also had trouble spelling the composer's name.

30 "Deep in my dark": Auden told Alan Ansen that this song, with its seven-syllable lines, was written in imitation of an Old Norse meter called *kviðuháttr*, as employed in the tenth-century skaldic poem *Sonatorrek*, by Egill Skallagrímsson. Auden discovered this poem in *Anglo-Saxon and Norse Poems*, edited by N. Kershaw (Cambridge: Cambridge University Press, 1922).

30 "*Bugs in the Bed* by *Bog Myrtle & Her Two-Timers*": See Auden's letter to Theodore Spencer (16 December 1946, *HUA*): "In any attempt to make contemporary figures symbolic, I think there has to be some quite [journalistically?] contemporary and hence dated stuff. I need the song-titles for this reason."

31 "The mutable circus": Ansen's typescript in the Berg reads, "variable," crossed through by Auden and replaced with "mutable."

As John Fuller has explained (*JF* 376–77), here Auden is representing theological disputation as a version of ancient Roman chariot racing. "Green and blue were the colours of the different racing factions. . . . The laps of each race were measured by movable eggs and dolphins (emblems of the horse gods Castor and Pollux, and Neptune)."

32 "*famus*": Perhaps a form of "*famulus*," a scholar's or magician's assistant.

32 "Commuters mimic the Middle Way": The Buddha counseled a "Middle Way" between the extremes of sensual gratification and strict asceticism.

32 "to a tidy fortune": Changed in the second Random House printing from "towards a tidy fortune."

32 "Persists somehow": Changed in the second Random House printing from "Persists that somehow that some day all this."

32 "The Night of the Knock": This seems to be an invocation of multiple moments of terror: the "night of the long knives," the 1934 purge of the Nazi Party that Auden refers to in his earlier long poem "New Year Letter"; *Kristallnacht*, the Nazis' November 1938 pogrom against German Jews; and, lying behind both, the Passover story, in which the children of Israel who daub their doors with blood are *spared* the Knock of the Angel of Death.

But perhaps more likely—given the reference to the "Absolute Instant" in the next line—is a reference to the Day of Judgment, which, Auden learned from both Eugen Rosenstock-Huessy and Kafka, is both an event at the end of history and an event that can happen at any time in the life of a person. In his book *The Prolific and the Devourer* (unpublished in his lifetime) Auden quotes Kafka: "Only our concept of time makes it possible for us to speak of the Day of Judgement by that name; in reality it is a summary court in perpetual session" (*P2* 433). Auden also cites this sentence in *The Viking Book of Aphorisms*.

In German the Day of Judgment is known as *Der Jüngste Tag*, the Youngest Day, and a few years after completing *The Age of Anxiety* Auden wrote, in the "Compline" section of "Horae Canonicae," "spare / Us in the youngest day when all are / Shaken awake" (*CP* 639).

35 "As life after life": Changed in the second Random House printing from "As life after life lapsing out of."

35 "Danaids": In Greek mythology, the fifty daughters of Danaus (also known as the Danaides). In punishment for killing their husbands, they were forced in the Underworld to try to carry water in sieves.

36 "William East is / Entering": Changed in the second Random House printing from "William East / Is entering."

36 "His cone-shaped skull": Ansen's typescript in the Berg reads, "The kings they have killed."

36 "In pay and prices, peregrinations": Changed in the second Random House printing from "the peregrinations."

36 "terminal god, / Tall by a torrent, the etruscan landscape / Of Man's Memory": Auden wrote an "Ode to Terminus"—the Roman god of boundaries,

and, Auden says, of "walls, doors, and reticence"—in 1968 (CP 811). Auden uses "etruscan" as a lowercase adjective, not a geographical reference: he may be alluding to the uniqueness of the Etruscan language—it is apparently unrelated to any other language—and the fact that it remains only imperfectly understood. These qualities are shared by each individual human memory.

Ansen's typescript in the Berg has "terminal god / Of Memory's fields. The myths of being. . . ." This is crossed out and the text of the published version written in by Auden.

37 "Polyphemus": The gigantic Cyclops Odysseus confronts in the *Odyssey* (bk. 12).

37 "Kind Orpheus": First printing omits "Kind." On several occasions Auden uses the word "kind" in its old sense of "natural": see his poem "Dame Kind" (i.e., Mother Nature: *CP* 665) and the first line of the first poem of the "Horae Canonicae": ". . . the kind / Gates of the body fly open . . ." (*CP* 625).

37 "virid": Green, verdant.

37 "Designed life": Changed in the second Random House printing from "Designed life, the presented picture / Is a case of chaos."

38 "He pines for some / Nameless Eden where he never was": See the Introduction, page xxiii above.

39 "Sir Ambrose Touch" etc.: There is a long history in English literature of absurd or ironic names of characters, from Shakespeare and Ben Jonson through Bunyan and Restoration comedy to modern favorites of Auden's, P. G. Wodehouse and Ronald Firbank. In a 1961 broadcast on Firbank Auden writes, "Consulting the Firbank telephone directory we find such names as: St Automona Meris, Lilian Bloater, Father Damien Forment, Lady Parvula de Panzoust, Lady Lucy Saunter, Eva Schnerb, Mrs Shamefoot, Monseigneur Silex, Sir Somebody Something, Guy Thin, Canon Wertnose, Madame Wetme, Mrs Yajñavalkya" (the BBC's *Listener,* 8 June 1961). Any number of these could find a place in *The Age of Anxiety.*

39 "Congested with gibbets": Changed in the second Random House printing from "Congested with gibbets; just as we reached / The monastery bridge the mist cleared / And I got one glimpse."

39 "the Good Place": Cf. Henry James's story "The Great Good Place" (1900), a story Auden referred to often in the 1940s. "Three impressions in particular had been with him all the week, and he could but recognise in silence their happy effect on his nerves. How it was all managed he couldn't have told—he had been content moreover till now with his ignorance of cause

and pretext; but whenever he chose to listen with a certain intentness he made out as from a distance the sound of slow sweet bells. How could they be so far and yet so audible? How could they be so near and yet so faint? How above all could they, in such an arrest of life, be, to *time* things, so frequent? The very essence of the bliss of Dane's whole change had been precisely that there was nothing now to time. It was the same with the slow footsteps that, always within earshot to the vague attention, marked the space and the leisure, seemed, in long cool arcades, lightly to fall and perpetually to recede. This was the second impression, and it melted into the third, as, for that matter, every form of softness, in the great good place, was but a further turn, without jerk or gap, of the endless roll of serenity. The quiet footsteps were quiet figures; the quiet figures that, to the eye, kept the picture human and brought its perfection within reach. This perfection, he felt on the bench by his friend, was now more within reach than ever."

40   "When we danced deisal": "Deisal" (also "deasil") means to turn continually to the right. "Vert" as an adjective is Auden's back-formation from the verb form that means "to turn in a particular direction or into an abnormal position"; The *OED* (2nd ed.), cites this line as the only instance of the adjectival form, referring to it as a poet's "nonce-word." "Volent" is riding at a gallop.

40   "Wafna": An expletive or curse taken from a mock liturgy in the *Carmina Burana*, the songs and poems attributed to the Goliards, the class of educated jesters and authors, some of them in holy orders, in the twelfth and thirteenth centuries: "*Wafna, wafna! quid fecisti, Sors turpissima?*" ("What have you done, foulest luck?") Auden commented to Alan Ansen that "'Wafna' comes from one of the Goliardic poems. It's an expression used in connection with a hangover" (*TT* 52).

41   "The Accuser": One of the core meanings of the Hebrew word "Satan," first used as a name in the prologue to Job, later identified by Jews and Christians with the Devil (e.g., Revelation 12:10), and prominent in the Zohar; cf. "the Adversary" in Auden's 1928 poem "Taller to-day" (*CP* 30).

41   "Homo Vulgaris, the Asterisk Man": Several times in his career Auden wrote poems that strive to encapsulate or summarize the historical development of humanity. The first large-scale attempt is in the sequence of poems first published as "In Time of War" (in the travel book he wrote with Christopher Isherwood, *Journey to a War* [1939]) and revised as "Sonnets from China" (*CP* 183–94). Another version is dispersed through "For the Time Being" (*CP* 347–400); and in 1949, soon after completing *The Age of Anxiety*, he would retell the saga in "Memorial for the City" (*CP* 589–94).

43 "There was Lord Lugar at Lighthazels": These persons and places are fictional, images from Rosetta's idealized and largely imaginary English childhood. See the Introduction, page xxii above.

45 "Come, peregrine nymph . . . delight your shepherds": The first overt appearance of the pastoral theme in this "eclogue." See the Introduction, page xxxviii above.

45 "the superior archons": Archons were the chief magistrates of the ancient Athenian republic, but here a more general way of identifying anonymous and forbidding powers.

45 "For the journey homeward / Arriving by roads already known": Changed in the second Random House printing from "For the journey home / Arriving by roads one already knows." Auden may have in mind here the end of Eliot's "Little Gidding":

> We shall not cease from exploration
> And the end of all our exploring
> Will be to arrive where we started
> And know the place for the first time.

Auden concluded a lecture at Swarthmore in 1943 by reading the whole stanza in which these lines are contained, calling Eliot "the greatest poet now living, . . . one whose personal and professional example are to every other and lesser writer at once an inspiration and a reproach" (*P2* 182).

46 "indagation": A searching out; an investigation.

46 "a landscape bearing a symbolic resemblance to the human body": In Ansen's typescript in the Berg this passage reads simply, "So it was now. The more completely. . . . " The intervening explanation is written on the typescript in Alan Ansen's hand. Clearly at this very late stage in the process of composition Auden had come to accept that the quest of "The Seven Stages" was going to be incomprehensible to many readers unless he gave them more guidance. See the Introduction, page xxviii above, and the schematic outline of the stages provided below.

PART THREE: THE SEVEN STAGES

Page

47 "Stages": Some critics have assumed that, given Auden's devotion to Kierkegaard, this must be a reference to the latter's book *Stages on Life's Way*

(1845). But there is nothing in this section that clearly resembles Kierke-gaard's delineation of the three stages—better, "spheres"—that he called the aesthetic, the ethical, and the religious.

Auden wrote to Alan Ansen about this part of the poem that "it's all in the Zohar": "It begins in the belly, the center of the body, goes on to the general region around the heart, then to the hands (symmetrically, two by two), then to the nose and throat (the capital), then north to the eyes where Rosetta goes in and the others describe it from outside, then to the forehead complex (museum), the ears (garden) through which one receives spiritual direction, the hair (woods), and finally they look down the back, the desert—there's nothing farther" (diary in the Berg; see also *LA* 251).

So a general schematic outline—derived from this letter plus some helpful commentary by John Fuller (*JF* 378–83)—might look like this:

stage	landscape	parts of the body
1	"a sad plain"	belly
	"peaks ... twin confederate forms"	breasts
2	"high heartland"	heart
	"railroads . . . rivers"	blood vessels
	"rival ports"	hands
3	"town . . . the capital"	head
4	"trolley car"	neurons
	"big house"	brain
	"window"	eyes
5	"the forgotten graveyard"	skull
6	"the hermetic gardens"	ears
	"the labyrinthine forest"	hair
7	"desert"	back

As one looks at this table, it is hard not to think of the scheme for *Ulysses* that Joyce provided for his friend Stuart Gilbert, which assigned or-gans of the body to fourteen of the seventeen episodes of the book. Like-wise, the imagery of *Finnegans Wake* figures the city of Dublin as the recum-bent body of a sleeping man: see John Gibson, *Joyce's Book of the Dark:* Finnegans Wake (Madison: University of Wisconsin Press, 1986), especially "Relief Map B," 34–35. Auden had read the *Wake* itself with the assistance of

Joseph Campbell and Henry Morton Robinson's *Skeleton Key to Finnegans Wake* (New York: Harcourt, 1944) soon after the latter book's publication and, therefore, near the beginning of his work on *The Age of Anxiety* (see *LA* 252).

47 "*O Patria, patria! Quanto mi costi!*": "O my country, my country! What you cost me!" Spoken by Aida in Verdi's opera: she is torn between the love of her native Ethiopia and her love of the Egyptian warrior Radames, who is likewise divided.

As with the epigraphs to other parts of the poem, this epigraph is written in Ansen's hand on Ansen's typescript in the Berg.

47 "Dotterels and dunlins": A dotterel is kind of plover, a dunlin a kind of sandpiper.

47 "tarn": A small mountain pond; the term is used especially in northern England, in the Lake District and the Pennines.

47 "oddling": An odd person; another northern English word.

48 "How still it is; our horses": This poem was first published, under the title "Noon," in *Silo* (Spring 1946). It was published as the first of "Three Dreams" in *W. H. Auden: A Selection by the Author* (Harmondsworth: Penguin, 1958); in the United States this volume appeared under the title *Selected Poetry of W. H. Auden* (New York: Modern Library, 1958). "Three Dreams" also appears in *CSP* (217).

For the Penguin selection, and the re-presentation of these speeches as "Three Dreams," Auden made several small changes that I have incorporated here; these are noted here and below.

In the first line of this speech, all editions before the Penguin selection read, "the horses"; likewise in the next line "our mothers" reads, "the mothers."

48 "And a freckled orphan": Changed in the Penguin selection from "the freckled orphan"; likewise "Ducks and drakes at a pond" was changed from "the pond." The comma at the end of that line seems ungrammatical, but Auden added it for the Penguin selection.

48 "Lugalzaggisi": An ancient Sumerian monarch whose name Auden picked up from Arnold Toynbee's *A Study of History*, which, as he told Christopher Isherwood in a letter, he was reading in the summer of 1944 (see *LA* 245).

48 "corresponsive": Slightly archaic variant of "corresponding."

49 "Lights are moving": In *CSP* this is the second of "Three Dreams"; see his comments on these lines in the Appendix, above.

49 "On domed hills": Changed in the Penguin selection of Auden's poems from "On the domed hills"; likewise in the next line "little monks" was changed from "the little monks."

49 "The vulgar lingo": Ansen's typescript in the Berg reads, "language," which Auden crosses out and replaces with "lingo."

49 "Bending forward": In *CSP*, the third of "Three Dreams."

50 "This stony pass": Ansen's typescript in the Berg reads, "This strong climb," which Auden crosses out and replaces with the published version.

51 "Danish buttons": In his unpublished essay on the poem (in the Berg Collection) Ansen explained "Danish buttons" on the basis of the entry for "Button" in the *Encyclopedia Britannica*, 11th ed. (1911), which reports that "about 1807 B. Sanders, a Dane who had been ruined by the bombardment of Copenhagen, introduced an improved method of manufacturing [a particular kind of button] at Birmingham." Replying to this conjecture on 27 August [1947], Auden wrote: "Danish buttons. I had no idea there were such things. Since however you say the inventor went to Birmingham, my home town, perhaps this is a forgotten memory" (Berg). Despite Ansen's ingenious suggestion, there seems to be no evidence that the buttons invented by Sanders in Birmingham were ever called Danish buttons, so Auden probably was right in thinking he had invented the term.

51 "Mariners Tavern": Robert Forsythe writes, "In the description of the Mariners Tavern and its accompanying stanza, the feeling that the author is familiar with the Tan Hill Inn and the view from Hartside [Hartside Fell, in Cumbria] is strong for anyone knowing that Auden had visited these locations" (*PP* 32).

55 "brim from belvederes": Ansen's typescript in the Berg reads, "robust on balconies," which Auden crosses out and replaces with the published version.

55 "And graceful dancing, gaze": Ansen's typescript in the Berg reads, "And stately balls there stand," which Auden crosses out and replaces with the published version.

56 "These ancient harbors": This and the following three stanzas were first published in *Inventario* (Autumn–Winter 1946–47) under the title "Landfall." The final stanza there begins with "And" rather than "As." See Auden's comment on the form used here in the Appendix, above.

56 "fucoid": Resembling seaweed.

59 "pyknics": One of the body types developed by the German psychiatrist Ernst Kretschmer, more or less equivalent to William Herbert Sheldon's "endomorph." Auden enjoyed playing with the idea that there are distinct somatotypes that correspond to psychological proclivities; in later poems and essays Sheldon's terms—endomorph, ectomorph, mesomorph—recur often.

59 "*filles-de-joie*": Prostitutes.

60 "The scene has all the signs": Malin's speech here was published in *Commonweal* (20 December 1946) under the title "Metropolis." Auden said that the city he had in mind here was Brussels (*JF* 381).

60 "dendritic": branching; also alludes to "dendrite" in the anatomical sense of a branch extending from a nerve cell.

61 "After thousands": Auden added this line by hand to Ansen's typescript in the Berg.

63 "Opera glasses on the ormolu table": Rosetta's speech here was published in the *New Yorker* (28 September 1946) under the title "Spinster's Song" (*JF* 381).

64 "Kibroth-Hattavah": In Hebrew this may mean "the graves of lust." In Numbers 11, some of the Israelites wandering in the wilderness grow tired of manna and eat quail instead, after which the Lord smites the people "with a very great plague. And he called the name of that place Kibroth-hattaavah: because there they buried the people that lusted."

In *Eric, or Little by Little* (1858)—a novel describing the apparently innocuous pastimes that lead young boys into corruption—Frederick William Farrar wrote, "Kibroth-Hattaavah! Many and many a young Englishman has perished there! Many and many a happy English boy, the jewel of his mother's heart—brave and beautiful and strong—lies buried there." In his *A Certain World: A Commonplace Book* (London: Faber & Faber, 1970), Auden cited this passage as an example of "Prose, Purple" (311).

64 "Yonder, look, is a yew avenue": Changed in the second Random House printing from "in" for "is."

65 "vetch and eyebright / And viper's bugloss": Common English plants. Vetch is a kind of legume; eyebright was once thought to strengthen weak eyes.

66 "Flittermice": Bats.

67 "QUANT mutters": The passage from this line through "Will your need be me?" was added to Ansen's typescript in the Berg as a typed insert.

69 "Lovelier would this": Ansen's typescript in the Berg reads, "How lovely would this," which Auden crosses out and replaces with the published version.

69 "the hermetic gardens": This may refer to *Hortulus Hermeticus* ("The Hermetic Garden"), a book published in 1627 by the Bohemian alchemist Daniel Stolz von Stolzenberg (known generally as Daniel Stolcius). It is a kind of emblem book, in which alchemical concepts are presented via complex engravings to which brief poems are appended. The Hermetic tradition—derived from the name of a legendary ancient sage, Hermes Trismegistus—is concerned with the preservation and selective transmission of esoteric knowledge.

69 "How tempting to trespass": These verses (through "wild cabaletta") were first published in *Changing World* (Summer 1947) under the title "Baroque."

69 "pursive": Short of breath.

70 "daedal": Maze or labyrinth.

70 "relievos": Italian for "relief," that is, a raised surface.

74 "Repugn": Resist, oppose, contend against.

74 "the Limping One": Folk tradition in many Christian lands says that the Devil limps, having been lamed when he was cast out of Heaven and crashed to the floor of Hell. Auden may also have been thinking of a passage from the Zohar in which the rabbis encounter a man described only as "the limping one" who mocks the ignorance of the sages and claims to have achieved supernatural powers simply through knowing the cry of Koheleth: "Vanity of vanities; all is vanity!" (Ecclesiastes 1:2). However, John Fuller thinks this may be a reference to the Button-Molder who comes near the end of *Peer Gynt* to take Peer's soul and melt it down in his ladle (*JF* 382).

76 "pinguid": Rich, fertile (an obsolete usage).

79 "Balbus": Perhaps an allusion to the Roman proconsul Lucius Cornelius Balbus, who built the theater of Balbus in Rome, no trace of which survived into modern times.

79 "The Nothing who nothings": From Martin Heidegger's *Was ist Metaphysik* (1929): "*Das Nichts nichtet.*" Interestingly, Heidegger also wrote in this essay that "*Die Angst offenbart das nichts*"—it is anxiety that reveals the nothing.

80 "Long Ada and her Eleven Daughters": Near Penrith in Cumbria there is a stone circle called Long Meg and Her Daughters; in "Their Last Will and Testament" in *Letters from Iceland* (1937) Auden and Louis MacNeice leave "Long Meg / and her nine daughters" to "Barbara Hepworth, sculptress" (*Pl* 365; see also *PP* 38).

80 "Pillicock Mound": In the storm scene of *King Lear* (3.4), Edgar as Poor Tom sings, "Pillicock sat on Pillicock-hill." Pillicock is also a slang word for penis.

81 "Saying this, they woke up": Cf. the last words of the first part of Bunyan's *The Pilgrim's Progress* (1678): "So I awoke, and behold it was a dream."

PART FOUR: THE DIRGE

Page

83 "*His mighty work for the nation*": When King Edward VII died in May of 1910, this poem was sold on the streets of London. A full quotation might clarify its relation to the poem that follows:

The will of God we must obey.
Dreadful—our King taken away
The greatest friend of the nation
Mighty monarch and protector.

Heavenly Father, help in sorrow
Queen-Mother, and them to follow,
How to do without him who has gone!
Pray help, help, and do lead us on.

Greatest sorrow England ever had,
When death took away our Dear Dad;
A king was he from head to sole,
Beloved by his people one and all.

His mighty work for the nation,
Strengthening peace and securing union
Always at it since on the throne
Has saved the country more than one billion.

This is from the text Auden provides in *The Oxford Book of Light Verse* (London: Oxford University Press, 1939), #297. It's likely that Auden found the poem in Robert Graves's *The English Ballad: A Short Critical Survey* (London: Ernest Benn, 1927), 117–18.

On Ansen's typescript in the Berg, this epigraph is written in by Ansen, but only after he had written and crossed out another one:

For men stood by the grave of man
The grave of Alexander the Proud:
They sang words without falsehood
Over the prince from fair Greece.

The lines are by Robin Flower, an English poet and scholar (1881–1946). Auden would have seen this poem in Walter de la Mare's anthology *Come Hither* (1923), "a collection which," he once wrote, "more than any book I have read before or since, taught me what poetry is" (*P2* 37). Ansen gets the first line of the poem wrong: it properly reads, "Four men stood by the grave of a man."

83 "some semi-divine stranger": See the Introduction, page xxxii above.

83 "Sob, heavy world": This poem was published under the title "Lament for a Lawgiver" in *Horizon* (March 1948). In the notebook at the Harry Ransom

Center, a draft of it—very close to the final version—appears in a portion of the notebook otherwise devoted to "The Seven Ages."

84 "Agrippa": Marcus Vipsanius Agrippa, the Roman statesman and general who won the Battle of Actium (31 BCE) for his father-in-law, Octavian, greatly strengthening Octavian's grip on the reins of empire.

84 "Its purgative path": Ansen's typescript in the Berg reads, "fugitive," which is surely a transcription error: "purgative" is substituted in Auden's hand.

PART FIVE: THE MASQUE

Page

87 "The Masque": A masque is a highly artificial theatrical entertainment that flourished in the seventeenth century. It typically combined a rudimentary plot with singing, dancing, instrumental music, and elaborate sets and costumes. It is a courtly genre, and often associated with courtly festivities: a wedding would be a proper occasion for a masque.

87 "'Oh, Heaven help me,' she prayed": See the Introduction, page xxxiii above. On Ansen's typescript in the Berg this is written in by Ansen.

87 "Human beings are, necessarily, actors": See the Introduction, page xxxiii above.

87 "Quaraquorams": Auden picked up these names from Toynbee's A Study of History (see LA 245).

88 "When Laura lay": These lines contain a series of double entendres based on the jargon of lead mining, as John Fuller explains: "'Laura' is a seam of ore, and her apparently nude posture merely a description of its accessibility to mining. . . . Ledger = lying horizontally; cheek = side of a vein; plight = fold; grove = mining shaft; random = direction of a vane; rise = working on the up side of a shaft" (JF 384).

88 "a Fen District": The low, marshy region of eastern England.

88 "Hushed is the lake of hawks": This beautiful lyric is Auden's attempt to use an Old Norse verse form called dróttkvaet. He seems to have been rather proud of this poem: he copied it out in a letter to Theodore Spencer (23 January 1946, HUA) and explained the metrical rules. In a later letter he called it "an attempt at a Drápa"—see the Appendix to this edition, above—but this is presumably an error: according to The New Princeton Dictionary of Poetry and Poetics (Princeton: Princeton University Press, 1993), a drápa is "an elaborate skaldic poem consisting of a number of stanzas in the same

metrical pattern"—one of the chosen patterns being *dróttkvaet*—"with a re-frain of two or more half-lines at regular intervals."

The poem employs kennings (for example, "lake of hawks" for the sky) to invoke each of the traditional four elements.

89 "Bold banners": Ansen's typescript in the Berg reads, "Banners blossom, meanings / Abound where love is found." These lines are crossed out by Auden and replaced with the final version. In a letter to Ansen dated 27 August (1947), replying to Ansen's draft essay on the poem, Auden wrote: "The drott-kwett. The first four kennings are the four elements. Banners of meaning, hosts of days are, so to speak, consciousness and history" (Berg).

89 "pelagic meadows": "Pelagic" refers to the open sea and its creatures; whales "graze" on plankton as cows on grass.

91 "the local spirits": Quant seems to be trying to make the furniture of an ordinary apartment into the Lares and Penates—household gods—of Roman tradition. What follows is a kind of pastoral epithalamion, but presented in an assertively contemporary idiom. Vitamin B3, or niacin, used to be known colloquially as "Vitamin PP"; "Face-in-the-wall" could be a mirror or a portrait; "Collywobbles" is a stomachache; "Cupboard-Love" is an old idiom for affection given only in hope of some reward.

92 "Innocent be all your indiscretions": Changed in the second Random House printing from "Harmless be."

92 "Attack their tissues": The first edition reads, "attach", probably a tran-scription error by Ansen; first corrected in the 1968 *Collected Longer Poems.*

93 "a staid monadnock, / On her peneplain": A peneplain is a low, flat plain produced by erosion; in such an environment any erosion-resistant rock will eventually stand forth as a hill or mountain, and such a hill is called a monadnock. Cf. Mount Monadnock in New Hampshire.

96 "A room with a view / For a shut-in soul": A nod to E. M. Forster's novel *A Room with a View* (1908); Auden admired Forster as a novelist and truth-teller, and wrote a sonnet dedicating *Journey to a War* to Forster (1939): see *CP* 194.

96 "Every night for the outgoing classes": Changed in the second Random House printing from "the outgoing sort."

98 "Parameters rule": Changed in the second Random House printing from "Perameters," a simple misspelling.

98 "I'll coffin you up till / You rule again": An ironic reference to Arthur, *Rex quondam, Rex futurae* ("the once and future king").

98 "our words touched / On Babylon's banks": Cf. Psalm 137: "By the rivers of Babylon, there we sat down, yea, we wept, when we remembered Zion."

99 "If ever you see / A fuss": Changed in the second Random House printing from "If you ever see." Note the implication that the persecution of Jews could happen in America.

99 "Rimmon's party": Naman the Syrian in 2 Kings 5 asks the Lord's pardon for following his master in bowing down before the false god Rimmon.

99 "Such hopes end?": The first printing ends this sentence with an exclamation point; presumably a simple mistake.

100 "Though I fly to Wall Street": Cf. Psalm 139: "If I ascend up into heaven, thou art there: if I make my bed in hell, behold, thou art there. If I take the wings of the morning, and dwell in the uttermost parts of the sea; Even there shall thy hand lead me, and thy right hand shall hold me."

100 "Should I hide away": Changed in the second Random House printing from "Though I hide away."

101 "Laburnum Crescent": Edward Mendelson notes that in Birmingham, where Auden grew up, there is no Laburnum Crescent but there are many other streets with the word "Laburnum" in them—more than in any other English city (*LA* 256n).

101 "That wouldn't work": Changed in the second Random House printing from "That wouldn't work. He won't pretend to . . ."

101 "the mythical scenes I make up": See the Introduction, page xxii above.

101 "My poor fat father": Among the several lines in Rosetta's speech that echo Anna Livia Plurabelle's words in the final passage of Joyce's *Finnegans Wake* (London: Penguin, 2000 [1939]): "And it's old and old it's sad and old it's sad and weary I go back to you, my cold father, my cold mad father, my cold mad feary father, till the near sight of the mere size of him, the moyles and moyles of it, moananoaning, makes me seasilt saltsick and I rush, my only, into your arms. . . . Carry me along, taddy, like you done through the toy fair! If I seen him bearing down on me now under whitespread wings like he'd come from Arkangels, I sink I'd die down over his feet, humbly dumbly, only to washup" (627–28). The word "Auden" famous appears as a single sentence elsewhere in the *Wake* (279).

101 "Moses will scold if": Changed in the second Random House printing from "Moses will scold / If . . ."

102 "Pharaoh": A reference to the Egyptian captivity of the Israelites (see the book of Exodus), matching the earlier references to the Babylonian captivity.

102 "*Shema' Yisra'el*": Ansen's typescript in the Berg has a more idiosyncratic transliteration of the *Shema*, the most important prayer in Judaism: "*Shmai Ysral. Adonai eloheim, Adonai ehad.*" But this is crossed out and replaced by the final version. Presumably Auden sought expert help. This is Deuteronomy 6:4: "Hear, O Israel: The Lord our God is one Lord."

PART SIX: EPILOGUE

Page

103 "*Some natural tears*": Written on Ansen's typescript in the Berg by Ansen. These are the last five lines of *Paradise Lost*, which definitively eliminate the Arcadian hope to return to the place of original innocence:

> Some natural tears they dropt, but wiped them soon;
> The world was all before them, where to choose
> Their place of rest, and Providence their guide:
> They, hand in hand, with wandering steps and slow,
> Through Eden took their solitary way.

Part Six is the only section of the poem that Auden substantially revised after Ansen made the Berg typescript around December 1946. One set of changes affects the arrangement of Malin's and Quant's stanzas at the start of this section; these are described immediately below. The other significant change affects the ending; this is described at the end of this section of notes.

In the typescript, the opening prose paragraph is followed by the speech heading for Malin's first stanza ("Sitting in the train") and the stanza itself: "Age softens the sense of defeat." This is followed by the speech heading for Quant's first speech ("Walking through the streets") and the first two stanzas of Quant's song, "When the Victory Powers" and "But peace was promised." Malin's next speech heading and stanza follow ("Do we learn from the past"), and then two stanzas of Quant's song that were omitted from the final text:

QUANT sang:
> Through some clerical error there were no cars for Mongolia
> Who was forced of course to take official umbrage;
> Hither-Asia, it was learned, spoke only Sumerian,
> So an interpreter was telegraphed for while they talked in
>   undertones.

> But finally they got going and the Phrygian delegate,
> Whose literary allusions delighted the cognoscenti,
> Huffed and puffed through his opening oration—
> "We must remember," he reminded them, "the Man-in-Swimming-
>   Trunks."

This was followed by Malin's "Both professor and prophet", then two more stanzas of Quant's song, both omitted from the published text:

QUANT sang:
> The secret sessions began seriously next morning
> In what was formerly the Museum of Fashion and Handicrafts,
> Where the ministers met to re-model humanity
> While husky specters haunted the corridors.
>
> Gondwana's whiskers were a wow with the stenographers;
> Bald Azerbaijan embarrassed his hostesses
> With his larval habits; the police got insomnia
> Keeping tabs on Tyre who had a taste for the waterfront.

This was followed by Malin's "Yet the noble despair," and then two of Quant's stanzas that appear separately in the published text ("The Laurentian Landshield" and "But there were sensible"), which are adjacent in the typescript. This is followed by Malin's "We're quite in the dark"; then the speech heading for Quant that begins "Quant had now reached the house", which is followed in the typescript by two stanzas, not one:

> Why, Miss ME, what's the matter? Must you go woolgathering?
> At least you might look as if you liked what I sing to you.
> One would think you would be thankful, but all you think of is
>   woodge–woodge
> With the other hacks . . . After all I've forgiven you.
> Once I was your wonder. How short-winded you've gotten.
> Come, Tinklebell, trot. Let's pretend you're a thoroughbred.
> Over the hill now into Abraham's Bosom.

"Woodge-woodge" seems to mean sexual activity; Ansen misread this as "wooy-wooy" in the Berg typescript, but Auden wrote in the correct reading. The word may be Auden's transcription of otherwise unrecorded slang, or it may be another term that he misheard; at the time this edition was prepared the only published usage indexed in Google Books was in a poem that Ansen wrote some years later: "when we're snuggling down to a little basic woodge-woodge" (*Contact Highs: Selected Poems, 1957–1987* [Chicago: Dalkey Archive Press, 1989], 38).

These lines are followed, as in the printed text, by "So saying" and the last of Malin's stanzas.

103 "When the Victory Powers": Like Rosetta's earlier meditation—"Four who are famous confer in a *schloss*" (see page 14 above)—this is probably an imaginary conference of temporal Powers rather than a specific historical reference.

104 "hepatoscopists": Hepatoscopy is the practice of divination by inspecting the entrails (especially the liver) of animals.

104 "Laurentian Landshield": A massive geologic shield that stretches from the Great Lakes through eastern and central Canada to the Arctic Ocean. The Tethys Ocean was a great sea of the Paleozoic era.

105 "The Duodecimal System": A numerical system with a base of twelve rather than our common ten. Ansen's typescript in the Berg reads, "The Sexagesimal System was agreed to unanimously," which Auden crosses out and replaces with the published version.

106 "Why, Miss *ME*": A "camp" phrase that Auden perhaps learned from Chester Kallman, or adapted from the "camp" practice of prefacing almost anything with "Miss."

106 "Abraham's Bosom": An image of Heaven, taken from Jesus' story of the rich man and Lazarus (Luke 16:22–23).

106 "for work and for war": These five words are added by Auden to Ansen's typescript in the Berg.

107 "*Clarté*": Eugen Rosenstock-Huessy used this word to indicate the core convictions and general philosophical outlook of the French Enlightenment (see *JF* 387).

107 "Bacchus or the Great Boyg or Baal-Peor": Bacchus is the Greek god of wine and intoxication; the Great Boyg is a monster in Ibsen's *Peer Gynt*, a play of special importance to Auden; Baal-Peor is a Canaanite deity whom some Israelites were tempted to worship, thereby angering the Lord (Numbers 25).

107 "galimatias": Babble, nonsense.

107 "Wanting our own way": In the Beinecke notebook, Auden first wrote "their," then crossed it out and replaced it with "our."

107 "Self-So": Auden seems to have gotten this phrase from Arthur Waley's translation and commentary *The Way and Its Power: Lao Tzu's Tao tê Ching and Its Place in Chinese Thought* (1934). There we read that the sage "teaches

things untaught, / Turning all men back to the things they have left behind, / That the ten thousand creatures may be restored to their Self-so" (LXIV). In other translations the word Waley renders as "Self-so" is given as "nature." The restoration of an ideal original nature now damaged—and not just human nature but also that of the "ten thousand creatures," the whole of creation—is in these lines presented as the work of Christ rather than the post-Confucian sage.

108 "ingressant": "Entering, in-going," according to the *OED* (2nd ed.), which calls it a "nonce-word" and gives as its only example this line. Presumably it was coined to indicate the opposite of "egress."

108 "Their own disorder": In a letter to Ansen, 27 August [1947], replying to Ansen's draft commentary on the poem, Auden wrote: "Malin's final lines. The source is not Galatians but Romans VIII.18–23, and XI.30–32. 'Their own disorder is their own punishment' comes almost verbatim from Augustine's Confessions."

108 "His World to come": Until a very late stage of composition, this speech continued without a break for a further thirteen lines, which survive in the Berg typescript but which Auden deleted before publication. The phrase "His World to come" has no punctuation at the end, and the remaining lines, which conclude the poem in Ansen's typescript, read:

> When creation shall give out another fragrance
> Nicer in our nostrils a novel sweetness
> From cleansed creatures in real accord together
> As a feeling fabric all flushed and intact,
> Phenomena and numbers announcing in one
> Multitudinous oecumenical song
> Their grand giveness of gratitude and joy,
> Peaceful and plural, their positive truth an
> Authoritative This, an authentic Now
> Where in love and in laughter each lives himself
> For, united in His Word, cognition and power,
> System and Order, are a single glory,
> His pattern is complete complex and our places safe.

In Ansen's typescript in the Berg these lines conclude the poem: there is no final prose passage. They are somewhat reminiscent of Caedmon's Hymn in celebration of Creation, one of the earliest surviving Anglo-Saxon poems (late seventh century).

Auden adapted these lines for the "Litany and Anthem for S. Matthew's Day" that he wrote for the Dedication and Patronal Festival of the Church of S. Matthew, Northampton, in England, which was performed on 21 September 1946. He wrote a new prose "Litany" followed by an "Anthem" in two parts. The first part of the anthem began with the line "PRAISE YE THE LORD" and continued with a slightly revised version of the thirteen omitted lines, beginning "Let the whole creation give out another sweetness" and continuing to the final line, ending "their places safe." The second part of the anthem began with the line "BLESS YE THE LORD," continuing with an abridged and adapted version of the closing lines of the published version of Malin's speech, reduced to thirteen lines, beginning "We elude Him, lie to Him," and continuing through "have mercy on them all."

The poem, with the first line "Let us praise our Maker, with true passion extol Him," appears under the title "Anthem" in *CP* 330.

These lines appear at the beginning of the Beinecke notebook, and that draft differs from the typescript in readings that would find their way into published versions of the poem. The typescript reads, "cleansed creatures," but in the notebook "creatures" is crossed out and replaced by "occasions"—the word that would appear in both the "Litany" and "Anthem." Likewise, where the typescript reads, "an authentic Now," the notebook, the "Litany," and "Anthem" all read, "an unthreatened Now."

108 "So thinking": A loose notebook page with a pencil draft of the closing prose narrative was in the collection of Robert A. Wilson and is now in the University of Delaware Library (information from Edward Mendelson).

108 "the actual world": "Poetry makes nothing happen," as Auden famously wrote in "In Memory of W. B. Yeats" (*CP* 246).

108 "creation lay in pain and earnest": Cf. Romans 8:22–23: "For we know that the whole creation groaneth and travaileth in pain together until now. And not only they, but ourselves also, which have the firstfruits of the Spirit, even we ourselves groan within ourselves, waiting for the adoption, to wit, the redemption of our body."